Prolegomena to the Study of Yeats's Plays

Prolegomena to the Study of Yeats's Plays

by

George Brandon Saul

Philadelphia
University of Pennsylvania Press

I. M.

FELIX EMANUEL SCHELLING
and
ALLAN WADE

Prefatory Note

This volume has been prepared in the conviction that Yeats's plays have yet to receive adequate consideration, and in a sharing of Padraic Colum's belief ("Poet's Progress . . .": *cit. inf.*) that they "represent the greatest amount of dramatic poetry given the English-speaking world since the close of the Elizabethan age." In so far as feasible, it follows the essential plan of the author's *Prolegomena to the Study of Yeats's Poems,* to which reference (as *Proleg. I*) is occasionally made. Based on the reasonably definitive *Collected Plays* (London: Macmillan, 1952; N.Y.: Macmillan, 1953—but copyright 1952, and by comparison with the English edition spattered with errors), it essays for each play (1) a correction of any error in final dating if such error exists; (2a) a full publication record, utilizing numbers corresponding to those in the list given below, followed (b) by a reference to Wade's *Bibliography* for every translation there recorded; (3) notations on first production if the play has had production; (4) a statement of what is known about dates of composition and relevant concerns; and (5) resolution of conceivable obscurities, reference to important critical comment, and pertinent suggestion of parallel passages. Citations are very brief and imply reference to the present note, "E" and "A" in the text discriminating English and American editions respectively. Explanatory notes on the individual plays are referenced according to 87A, below.

7

A few notes on discarded or unpublished plays are assigned to an appendix.

The reference list follows of Yeats's volumes containing one or more of his plays, with detailed dating wherever confusion might threaten and asterisking of volumes with especially useful appendixes or notes; it includes one item (29a) of special corollary interest.

1. *Mosada. A Dramatic Poem.* Dublin, 1886.—V. Items 84 and 88, *inf.*
2. *The Wanderings of Oisin and Other Poems.* London, 1889.
2a. *The Wanderings of Oisin / Dramatic Sketches / Ballads / & / Lyrics.* London, 1892.
3. *The Countess Kathleen and Various Legends and Lyrics.* London, Sept. 1892; Boston & London, 1892.
4. *The Land of Heart's Desire.* London, Apr. 1894; Chicago, 1894.
5. ———. [Rev. version.] *Bibelot,* Portland, Me., July 1903; as separate vol., Oct. 1903 and later (Wade, *Biblio.,* It. 13, mentions a 12th ed. in Nov. 1916).
6. *Poems.* London, 1895; London & Boston, 1895.
7. *Poems* [1895]. Rev. eds., London, 1899, 1901, 1904, 1908, 1912, 1913, 1919, 1920, 1922 (2), 1923, 1924, 1927, 1929.
8. *The Shadowy Waters.* London, Dec. 1900, 1901; N.Y., 1901, 1901, 1905.
9. *Cathleen Ni Hoolihan.* London, Oct. 1902.
10. *Where There Is Nothing.* Supplement to *The United Irishman,* 1 Nov. 1902.
11. ———. Two ltd. eds. printed at New Rochelle, N.Y., for John Quinn, 1902.

12. ———: *Being Volume One of Plays for an Irish Theatre*. London, May 1903; N.Y. and London, 1903.

13. *In the Seven Woods*. Dundrum (*Dun Emer*), Aug. 1903 (though finished 16 July).

14. ———. N.Y. & London, 1903.

15. *The Hour-Glass*. London, 1903.

16. *The Hour-Glass and Other Plays* [Vol. II, "Plays for an Irish Theatre"]. N.Y. & London, 13 Jan. 1904, 1904, 1906 + ltd. 1904 ed.

17. *The Hour-Glass, Cathleen Ni Houlihan, The Pot of Broth*. . . . London, 1904.

18. ——— [Vol. IV, "Abbey Theatre Series"]. Dublin, 1905.

19. *The King's Threshold*. N.Y.: "Printed for Private Circulation," 1904: 2 eds.

20. *The King's Threshold: and On Baile's Strand* [Vol. III, "Plays for an Irish Theatre"]. London, 1904.

21. *The King's Threshold* [Vol. V, "Abbey Theatre Series"]. Dublin, 1905.

22. *On Baile's Strand* [Vol. VI, "Abbey Theatre Series"]. Dublin, 1905.

23. *The Pot of Broth*. London, 1905, 1911.

24. *Cathleen Ni Houlihan*. London, 1906, 1909; Stratford-upon-Avon, 1911.

25. *Poems, 1899–1905*. London & Dublin, 1906.

26. *The Shadowy Waters* [Acting version, showing Lady Gregory's hand in prose passages]. London, 1907.

27. *The Hour-Glass*. London, 1907.—V. Wade, *Biblio.*, It. 67, on two other supposed eds.

28. *On Baile's Strand*. London, 1907.—First separate issue of rev. version of 25.

29. *Deirdre* [Vol. V, "Plays for an Irish Theatre"]. London, Aug. 1907.—Cp. Wade, *Biblio.*, It. 69.

29a. *Alterations in "Deirdre."* Leaflet, London, Nov. 1908.

*30. *The Poetical Works of William B. Yeats*, Vol. II, Dramatical Poems. N.Y. & London, 8 July 1907 ("Preface" dated Dec. 1906), 1909, 1911.

31. *The Unicorn from the Stars and Other Plays by William B. Yeats and Lady Gregory.* N.Y., 13 May 1908, 1915.

32. *The Golden Helmet.* N.Y., 1908.

*33. *The Collected Works in Verse and Prose of William Butler Yeats.* Stratford-on-Avon, 1908.—Vol. II (Sept.): *The King's Threshold. On Baile's Strand. Deirdre. Shadowy Waters* [with "Acting Version" in App. I].

*33a. ———. Vol. III (Oct.): *The Countess Cathleen. The Land of Heart's Desire. The Unicorn from the Stars.*

*33b. ———. Vol. IV (Oct.): *The Hour-Glass. Cathleen Ni Houlihan. The Golden Helmet. The Irish Dramatic Movement.*

34. *The Land of Heart's Desire.* N.Y., 1909.

35. *Poems: Second Series.* London & Stratford-on-Avon, Mar. 1910, 1913.

36. *The Green Helmet and Other Poems.* Dundrum (*Cuala*), Dec. 1910 (though finished 30 Sept.).

37. *The Green Helmet and Other Poems.* N.Y., 16 Jan. 1911.

38. *Deirdre.* Stratford-upon-Avon, July 1911.

39. *The Green Helmet.* Stratford-upon-Avon, Nov. 1911.

40. *The King's Threshold.* Stratford-upon-Avon, Nov. 1911.

*41. *Plays for an Irish Theatre.* London & Stratford-upon-Avon, Dec. 1911, 1913.

42. *The Countess Cathleen.* London, June 1912.

43. *The Land of Heart's Desire* [Vol. II, "Dublin Plays"]. London, June 1912; later impressions, sometimes in variant binding, 1913, 1916, 1919, 1922 (2), 1923, 1924 (5), 1925; new ed., Paulton & London, 1937 [for 1927?—*v.* Wade, *Biblio.*, It. 94].

*44. *The Poetical Works of William B. Yeats.* Vol. II, Dramatic Poems. Rev., N.Y. & London, 7 Aug. 1912; rpt. N.Y. & London, 1914, 1916, 1917, 1919, 1921.

45. *The Green Helmet and Other Poems.* N.Y. & London, 23 Oct. 1912.

46. *A Selection from the Poetry of W. B. Yeats.* Leipzig (Tauchnitz), (? Jan.) 1913 ("Preface" dated Oct. 1912), 1922.

47. *The Hour Glass.* Pvtly. printed (*Cuala*), Jan. 1914. —New version, from *The Mask.*

48. *Responsibilities: Poems and a Play.* Dundrum (*Cuala*), 25 May 1914 (though finished May Eve).

49. *Deirdre.* Stratford-upon-Avon, 1914.

50. *The King's Threshold.* Stratford-upon-Avon, 1915.

51. *Responsibilities and Other Poems.* London, 10 Oct. 1916, 1917; N.Y., 1916.

52. *The Wild Swans at Coole.* Dundrum (*Cuala*), 17 Nov. 1917 (though finished 10 Oct.).

53. *The Well of Immortality* [*At the Hawk's Well*]. No printer's name, n.d.—*V.* Wade, *Biblio.*, It. 119.

54. *Two Plays for Dancers.* Dundrum (*Cuala*), Jan. 1919.

55. *The Land of Heart's Desire.* Boston, 1920.

*56. *Four Plays for Dancers.* London & N.Y., 1921.—Five of the lyrics rptd. in *Selected Poems,* London, 1929, 1930, 1932.

57. *Seven Poems and a Fragment.* Dundrum (*Cuala*), June 1922 (though finished in Apr.).

58. *Later Poems.* London, 3 Nov. 1922, 1922.

*59. *Plays in Prose and Verse.* London, 3 Nov. 1922 ("Coll. Ed." & "Cardinal Series"), 1922, 1926, 1930; N.Y., 1924; ltd. N.Y. ed., 1924.

60. *The Player Queen.* London, 21 Nov. 1922.

*61. *Plays and Controversies.* London, 27 Nov. 1923, 1927; N.Y., trade & ltd. eds., 1924.

62. *Later Poems.* Rev. eds., London, 1924, 1926, 1931.

63. *Later Poems.* N.Y., 8 Apr. 1924, 1928.

64. Combined eds. of *The Countess Cathleen & The Land of Heart's Desire.* London, 1924, 1925, 1929: *v.* Wade, *Biblio.,* It. 95.

65. *The Cat and the Moon and Certain Poems.* Dublin (*Cuala*), July 1924 (though finished 1 May).

66. *The Land of Heart's Desire.* San Francisco, 1926.

67. *Sophocles' King Oedipus.* London & N.Y., 1928.

68. *Stories of Michael Robartes and His Friends.* Dublin (*Cuala*), Mar. 1932 (though finished All-hallows Eve 1931).

69. *The Collected Poems of W. B. Yeats.* N.Y., 14 Nov. 1933 + 15 rptgs. through 1949.

70. *The Collected Poems of W. B. Yeats.* London, 1933, 1934, 1935, 1937, 1939.

71. *The Words upon the Window Pane.* Dublin (*Cuala*), Apr. 1934 (though finished late Jan.).

*72. *Wheels and Butterflies.* London, 13 Nov. 1934 ("Preface" dated 4 Aug.); N.Y., 1935.

73. *The Collected Plays of W. B. Yeats.* London, 30 Nov. 1934; N.Y., 1935 (copy. '34).

74. *The King of the Great Clock Tower.* Dublin (*Cuala*), 14 Dec. 1934 (though finished in Oct.).

75. *The King of the Great Clock Tower.* N.Y., 1935.

76. *A Full Moon in March.* London, 22 Nov. 1935.

77. *The King's Threshold.* London, 25 Mar. 1937.

78. *Nine One-Act Plays.* London, 8 June 1937.

79. *The Herne's Egg.* London, 21 Jan. 1938.

80. *The Herne's Egg and Other Plays.* N.Y., 12 Apr. 1938.

81. *Last Poems and Two Plays.* Dublin (*Cuala*), 10 July 1939 (though finished June).

82. *On the Boiler.* Dublin (*Cuala*), 1939 ("Preface" dated Oct. 1938), 1939.

83. *Last Poems & Plays.* London (Jan.) and N.Y., 1940; N.Y., 1940.

84. *Mosada.* Dublin: Pvtly. Printed (*Cuala*), 1943.— Corrected ed.

85. *The Poems of W. B. Yeats,* Vol. I. London, 25 Nov. 1949.

86. *The Collected Poems of W. B. Yeats.* London, 4 July 1950, 1952, 1954; N.Y., 1951, 1951 (with several corrections), 1951, 1952, 1953, 1954, 1955, 1956 (with revisions to bring correspondence with 85: *v. Proleg. I*).

87. *The Collected Plays of W. B. Yeats.* London, 1952; N.Y., 1953.

88. *The Variorum Edition of the Poems of W. B. Yeats,* ed. P. Allt and R. K. Alspach. N.Y., 1957. (*Variorum*)

Other volumes by Yeats that receive mention are referenced according to the following editions and indicated abbreviations:

The Autobiography of William Butler Yeats. N.Y.: Macmillan, Issue of 1953. (*Auto.*)

Essays. N.Y.: Macmillan, 1924.

Essays, 1931 to 1936. Dublin: Cuala Press, 1937.

John Sherman and Dhoya [under pseudonym "Ganconagh" ("Love-talker")]. London: Unwin, 1891.

The Letters of W. B. Yeats, ed. A. Wade. N.Y.: Macmillan, 1955. (Wade)

Letters on Poetry . . . , ed. D. Wellesley. N.Y.: Oxford Univ. Press, 1940. (Wellesley)

Pages from a Diary Written in Nineteen Hundred and Thirty. Dublin: Cuala Press, 1944. (*1930 Diary*)

The Secret Rose. London: Lawrence & Bullen, Ltd., 1897.

A Vision. N.Y.: Macmillan, 1956.

W. B. Yeats: Letters to Katharine Tynan, ed. R. McHugh. N.Y.: McMullen, 1953. (McHugh)

Asterisked items excepted, the following works are cited by author's surname and (where necessary) page only, or by journal in the case of anonymous authorship:

Adams, H. "Yeats's *Country of the Young.*" *PMLA,* LXXII, 3 (June 1957), 510-19.

Anon. "Sophocles, Yeats and Dr. Gogarty." N.Y. *Herald Tribune,* 15 Jan. 1933.

———. "Yeatsian Fantasy." London *Times Lit. Supp.,* 22 Jan. 1938, p. 56.

Becker, W. "The Mask Mocked. . . ." *Sewanee Rev.*, LXI (1953), 82-108.

Beerbohm, M. "In Dublin." *Sat. Rev.*, LXXXVIII, 2272 (13 May 1899), 586-88.

*————. "Some Irish Plays and Players." *Sat. Rev.*, XCVII, 2528 (9 Apr. 1904), 455-57.

Bentley, E. "Yeats as a Playwright." *Kenyon Rev.*, X, 2 (Spr. 1948), 196-208.

Bjersby, B. *The Interpretation of the Cuchulain Legend in the Works of W. B. Yeats.* Upsala: Lundequistska Bokhandeln, Copenhagen: Monksgaard, & Dublin: Hodges, Figgis, 1950.

Block, H. M. "Yeats's *The King's Threshold*: The Poet and Society." *Philol. Qu.*, XXXIV (1955), 206-18.

Bottomley, G. "His Legacy to the Theatre." *The Arrow,* Summer 1939, 11-14.

*Boyd, E. *Contemporary Drama of Ireland.* Boston: Little, Brown, 1917. (*CDI*)

————. *Ireland's Literary Renaissance.* Rev. ed., N.Y.: Knopf, 1922.

Brewer's Dictionary of Phrase & Fable. London: Cassell, ed. 1953.

Colum, P. "Poet's Progress: W. B. Yeats in the Theatre." *Theatre Arts Mthly*, XIX (Dec. 1935), 936-43.

————. Rev. of *Selected Poems* (1921). *Dial*, LXXI (1921), 464.

Cross, T. P. *Motif-Index of Early Irish Literature.* Bloomington: Indiana Univ., 1952.

Curtis, E. *A History of Ireland.* N.Y.: Van Nostrand, n.d. [*c*. 1936].

Dume, T. L. *William Butler Yeats: A Survey of His Reading.* Unpub. Temple Univ. Diss., 1950.

Ellis-Fermor, U. *The Irish Dramatic Movement*. London: Methuen, 1939.

Ellmann, R. *Yeats / The Man and the Masks*. N.Y.: Macmillan, 1948.

*———. *The Identity of Yeats*. London: Macmillan, 1954. (*Iden.*)

Ferguson, D. N. *A History of Musical Thought*. N.Y.: Crofts, 1935.

Gogarty, O. St. J. *It Isn't This Time of Year at All!* Garden City: Doubleday, 1954.

Gregory, Lady I. A. *Cuchulain of Muirthemne*. N.Y.: Scribner's, 1902.

*———. *Our Irish Theatre*. N.Y.: Putnam, 1913. (*OIT*)

Griffin, G. *The Wild Geese*. London: Jarrolds, 1938.

Guthrie, W. N. "W. B. Yeats." *Sewanee Rev.*, IX, 3 (July 1901), 328-31.

*Gwynn, D. *Edward Martyn and the Irish Revival*. London: Cape, 1930.

Gwynn, S. *Irish Literature and Drama*. . . . London: Nelson, 1936.

*———. "Poetry and the Stage." *Fortnightly Rev.*, LXXXV, 506 (Feb. 1909), 337-51.

*———, ed. *Scattering Branches*. N.Y.: Macmillan, 1940.

Henn, T. R. *The Lonely Tower*. London: Methuen, 1950.

Hoare, D. M. *The Works of Morris and of Yeats in Relation to Early Saga Literature*. Cambridge: Cambridge Univ. Press, 1937.

Hone, J. M. *W. B. Yeats, 1865–1939*. N.Y.: Macmillan, 1943.

*———, ed. *J. B. Yeats' Letters to His Son*. . . . London: Faber and Faber, 1944.

*Hyde, D. *Beside the Fire*. London: Nutt, 1890.

————. *A Literary History of Ireland.* N.Y.: Scribner's, 1899.

Jeffares, A. N. *A Poet and a Theatre.* Groningen: Wolters, 1946.

Kavanagh, P. *The Story of the Abbey Theatre.* N.Y.: Devin-Adair, 1950.

Keating, G. *The History of Ireland.* Vol. I, ed. D. Comyn. London: Nutt, for Irish Texts Soc'y, 1902.—II, ed. P. S. Dinneen, 1908.

Macalister, R. A. S., ed.-trans. *Two Irish Arthurian Romances.* Irish Texts Soc'y, Vol. X [1907]. London: Nutt, 1908.

McGreevy, T. H. "Mr. W. B. Yeats as a Dramatist." *Revue Anglo-Américaine,* VII (1929–30), 19-36.

MacManus, S. *The Story of the Irish Race.* N.Y.: Devin-Adair, rpt. of 1945.

MacNamara, B. *Abbey Plays / 1899–1948.* Dublin: At the Sign of the Three Candles, n.d. [1949].

MacNeice, L. "Yeats's Epitaph." *New Republic,* CII, 26 (24 June 1940), 862-63.

Malone, A. E. *The Irish Drama, 1896–1928.* London: Constable, 1929.

Mills, J. G. "W. B. Yeats and Noh." *Japan Qu.,* II (1955), 496-500.

*Moore, G. *Hail and Farewell*—I: "Ave," II: "Salve." N.Y.: Appleton, 1911, 1914. (*H&F*)

Moore, V. *The Unicorn.* N.Y.: Macmillan, 1954.

"O'Connor, Frank" (Michael O'Donovan). "A Lyric Voice in the Irish Theatre." N.Y. *Times Book Rev.,* 31 May 1953, pp. 1, 16.

Parkinson, T. "W. B. Yeats: A Poet's Stagecraft, 1899–1911." *ELH,* XVII (1950), 136-61; or Ch. II, *W. B.*

Yeats / Self-Critic. Berkeley & Los Angeles: Univ. of Calif. Press, 1951.

Peacock, R. *The Poet in the Theatre.* N.Y.: Harcourt, Brace, 1946.

Pearce, D. R. "Yeats' Last Plays: An Interpretation." *ELH,* XVIII (1951), 67-76.

Pollock, J. H. *William Butler Yeats.* London: Duckworth & Dublin: Talbot Press, Ltd., 1935.

Reid, F. *W. B. Yeats / A Critical Study.* London: Secker, 1915.

Reinert, O. "Yeats' *The Hour-Glass.*" *Explicator,* XV (1956), It. 19.

Roberts, R. E. "W. B. Yeats, Dramatist." *New Statesman and Nation,* X (2 Nov. 1935), 636-37.

Robinson, L. *Curtain Up.* London: Michael Joseph Ltd., 1942.

*————. *Ireland's Abbey Theatre.* London: Sidgwick and Jackson, 1951. (*IAT*)

*————., ed. *The Irish Theatre.* London: Macmillan, 1939. (*IT*)

*————. *Lady Gregory's Journals, 1916–1930.* N.Y.: Macmillan, 1947. (*LGJ*)

*———— and T., and Dorman, Nora [Robinson]. *Three Homes.* London: Michael Joseph Ltd., 1938. (*TH*)

Rossi, M. M. "Yeats and Philosophy." *Cronos,* I (Fall 1947), 19-24.

Ryan, Sister M. Rosalie. *Symbolic Elements in the Plays of William Butler Yeats, 1892–1921.* (Diss.) Washington: Catholic Univ. of America Press, 1952.

*Saul, G. B. *Prolegomena to the Study of Yeats's Poems.* Philadelphia: Univ. of Pa. Press, 1957. (*Proleg. I*)

————. *The Shadow of the Three Queens.* Harrisburg: Stackpole, 1953.

Sampson, G. *The Concise Cambridge History of English Literature*. Cambridge: Cambridge Univ. Press & N.Y.: Macmillan, 1941.

Smaller Classical Dictionary, A, ed. from Smith by E. H. Blakeney. "Everyman's Library." London: Dent & N.Y.: Dutton, rpt. of 1917.

Strong, L. A. G. *A Letter to W. B. Yeats*. London: Hogarth Press, 1932.

Suss, I. D. "Yeatsian Drama and the Dying Hero." *So. Atlan. Qu.*, LIV (1955), 369-80.

Suzuki, B. L. *Nōgaku.* . . . London: Murray, 1932.

Thompson, F. J. "Ezra in Dublin." *Univ. of Toronto Qu.*, XXI (1951–52), 64-77.

Tindall, W. Y. *Forces in Modern British Literature*. N.Y.: Knopf, 1947.

Tynan, K. *The Middle Years*. Boston & N.Y.: Houghton Mifflin, 1917.

Ure, P. *Towards a Mythology.* . . . Liverpool: Univ. Press & London: Hodder and Stoughton, 1946.

*Wade, A. *A Bibliography of the Writings of W. B. Yeats*. London: Hart-Davis, 1951. (Wade *Biblio.*)

Weygandt, C. *Irish Plays and Playwrights*. Boston: Houghton Mifflin, 1913.

Wilde, Lady F. *Ancient Legends . . . of Ireland.* . . . London: Chatto & Windus, ed. 1902.

Wilson, F. A. C. *W. B. Yeats and Tradition*. London: Gollancz, 1958.

I should remark that broadly general and comprehensive studies of the plays usually receive mention in reference to individual plays only if they seem to contribute some special illumination or key to history or interpretation. Dr. Bjersby's book should be considered, of course, in relation to all the Cuchulain plays.

ACKNOWLEDGMENTS

I wish to thank Dr. Delvin L. Covey, of the University of Connecticut, for checking and in some cases revising my translations of the Latin passages in *The Hour-Glass;* Miss Roberta Smith, reference librarian of the Wilbur Cross Library, University of Connecticut, for gracious services in borrowing books and periodicals necessary to the completion of this work; Mr. Padraic Colum, for several helpful suggestions; and Mr. Denis Johnston, for generous aid in identifying some of the place-names found in the plays.
March 1958.

Contents

Prolegomena to the Study of
Yeats's Plays

THE COUNTESS CATHLEEN

1: The version in 87 is the final *reading* version, with original publication correctly dated 1892; except for very minor alterations, this version is the same as those of 61 and 73: it is not the Abbey acting version, which differs from the point where the Merchants disappear (87A, 28).—The best text (1957) is that of 87E.

2a: 3 (*The Countess Kathleen*), 6 (. . . *Cathleen*): rev., 7: rev. (and again in its 1899, 1901, and 1912 rptgs.), 30, 33a, 42: rev.—opening two scenes markedly, latter portion in some degree: valuable notes (rptd. in 61—A, 285-95), 44, 46, 61: rev., 64, 73, 87.—*N.B.* The song in Sc. V appeared as "Kathleen," *Nat'l Observer*, 31 Oct. 1891. The revisions and notes of 42 follow those of the seventh edition of 6, which also introduces the new ending of the acting version first played at the Abbey 14 Dec. 1911.

b: V. Wade *Biblio.*, 352, 353, 354, 356, 357, 358, 360, 362, 363, 370.

3: 8 May 1899; Antient Concert Rooms, Great Brunswick (>Pearse) St., Dublin; by "Irish Literary Theatre."—For cast, history, and revision, *v.* "Note," 61 (A, 290 ff.); Lady Gregory, *OIT*, 20-25; Robinson, *IAT*, 5-12.—On early Roman Catholic opposition, etc., *v.* Wade, 316-20, 350; Hone, 167-70; *Auto.*,

25

250 ff., 271-72; Yeats's letter, "The Countess Cathleen and Cardinal Logue," *Morning Leader,* 13 May 1899; Gwynn, 152-53; Jeffares, 8-9; Moore, *H&F,* I, §§ II and III.—*En passant,* cp. Joyce's *Portrait of the Artist as a Young Man,* § 5.

4: Maud Gonne had urged Yeats to write a play; and she, with her work among the Donegal poor (Hone, 100; Jeffares, 5-6), became the imaginary heroine of this one, with Yeats himself the original of Aleel.— The play was begun early in 1889 (cp. Wade, 114, 125); "half written" by 13 July 1889 (*Idem,* 129); still in process two years later (*Idem,* 173); and finished Oct. 1891.—On its source, *v.* 61 (A, 285 ff.) and Wade, 346. Robinson (*Scattering Branches,* ed. Gwynn) says the song in Sc. II was inspired by a London visit of the Russian ballet.—By 1894, Yeats was at work on a revision, finished before Christmas of that year (Hone, 118); important further revision was undertaken early in 1912 (Wade, 567; on the concluding tableau, *v. 1930 Diary,* 19; cp. also Henn, 108-10).

This, which George Moore (Wade, 271) called "the finest verse play written since Shakespeare," may conceivably have been Yeats's favorite among his own plays: cp. the preface to *Plays and Controversies,* and *v.* also pp. 63 and 89 (A) of that volume. Yeats's published correspondence contains more references to this than to any of his other plays.

In his "Preface to the Fourth Edition" (*v.* Appendix to 33a), Yeats admits his "pleasure in stage effects" when he first wrote this play; the numerous revisions involved in shaping it from a four-act into a five-scene work were fully justified except for the loss

(Act III) of Cathleen's "I know of nothing but a harp-string / That can remember happiness." Originally both dialogue and action were romanticized to a degree that weakened dramatic impact, and the purely decorative was overstressed: e.g., Cathleen, Oona, and Aleel were accompanied by a group of musicians; Shemus crushed a household shrine of the Virgin when it fell at one of his remarks; the demons began by making Shemus and Teig drunk; a priest died—apparently of fright; sea dwarfs and dead folk were introduced, though for no significant purpose; etc.—Incidentally, *Morian* (*v.* title page) is prior to 73 spelled *Morion*.

5: *Gloss*:

P. 2, l. 4: Tubber-vanach: Really Tubber?—V. gloss to *The Pot of Broth*.

l. 8: Carrick-orus: Imaginary?—Denis Johnston suggests in a personal letter a possible combination of Carrickmines and Ballycorus (Co. Dublin).

P. 5, l. 5: Cp. "The Fiddler of Dooney" (85, 86, or 88) and *Proleg. I*.

P. 6, l. 6: Cp. "If music be the food of love, play on": *Twelfth Night*, l. 1.

P. 7, l. 29: "all but nothing": 42 reads "but a straw."

P. 8, l. 12: "who" = "whom."

P. 10, l. 8: "Is fancy bread": 42 has—more logically?—"Is fancy bred."

P. 11, l. 11: Maeve: Medb, wild queen of Connacht, sometimes, as here, reputed queen of the elf-folk; cp. Saul, 78 ff.

l. 22: Knocknarea (*Cnoc-na-righ*: "Mountain

of the King"): Mountain in Sligo, its top supposedly the site of Medb's cairn. Cp. "The Wanderings of Oisin," ll. 17-18, and "Red Hanrahan's
Song about Ireland" (85, 86, or 88).

P. 12, ll. 17-18: Cp. Cross, F300 *et seq.* (pp. 255 ff.)

P. 13, l. 16: Cro-Patrick: Croagh Patrick, in southwestern Mayo: With Lough Derg, one of the two
great traditional Irish centers of Christian pil-
grimage; *v.* "Words for Music . . . ," XXI (85, 86,
or 88), and *Proleg. I.*

P. 14, ll. 5 ff.: Cp. "Paudeen" (85, 86, or 88):
"There cannot be . . . / A single soul that lacks
a sweet crystalline cry."

P. 16, l. 12: Œngus (Aengus): Celtic god of love
and beauty (Saul, 21), the birds his transformed
kisses.

P. 17, l. 26: "her": Virgin Mary.

Pp. 18-19: The Merchants' speeches through l. 8,
p. 19, replace over eight pages of the 1912 text.

P. 18, l. 13: "Country-under-Wave":   *Tir-fa-tonn:*
Name reflecting one Celtic concept of the Otherworld; cp. "Under the Moon" (85, 86, or 88).

P. 19, l. 18: "bog of Allen": Allen is legendary Alm-
hain (Almhuin), Co. Kildare, Finn Mac Cum-
hall's center.

l. 19: Fair Head: A point on N coast of Co.
Antrim, E of Ballycastle Bay.

P. 21, l. 10: "Ochone!" — "Alas!"

P. 23, l. 13: Donegal: A county in NW Ireland.

l. 18: "in like feathers": i.e., also as an owl.

l. 19: Meath: E coast county, N of Dublin;
anciently *Mide,* with its capital, Tara, the seat of
the High Kings of Ireland.

P. 27, Sec. Merchant's third speech: Griffin (158-59) says Cardinal Logue counted these lines an "insidious attack on the line of popes from Saint Peter to Leo XIII. . . ."—Cp. *Auto.*, 252.

P. 28, l. 16: Balor: Monstrous Fomorian king; cp. "The Wanderings of Oisin," III (85, 86, or 88); Saul, 58, and *Proleg. I.*

l. 18: "eyes": The legendary Balor had only one.

l. 19: Barach: Conchubar's pawn in "The Fate of the Children of Usna"; cp. Saul, 76.

l. 20: Cailitin: Calatin, wizard, Ulster Cycle of Irish story; cp. Saul, 83.

l. 22: The child is Cuchulain (originally "Setanta").

l. 23: The king is Conchubar of Uladh (mod. Ulster).

l. 24: Naoise and Deirdre are the tragic hero and heroine of "The Fate of the Children of Usna": cp. Saul, 74 ff.

l. 25: Sr. M. Rosalie Ryan (41 fn. 6) glosses Dante's *Inferno*, XX.

P. 29, l. 2: Ryan (*loc. cit.*) glosses *Inferno*, XXXIV.

l. 6: Orchil: A queen of the Celtic Under-world. Cp. "The Madness of King Goll" (85, 86, or 88) and *Proleg. I.*

l. 12: Ryan (*loc. cit.*) glosses *Inferno*, V.

P. 31, l. 11: Moytura ("Flowery Plain"): The reference is specifically to the "Second Battle of Moytura," recorded in the Mythological Cycle of Irish story, wherein Balor lost his "death-pouring" eye: *v.* Saul, 58-59.

Yeats's father—for once inept in judgment—felt this play, which Griffin (159) says James Joyce translated into Italian and which in 1924 won its author the Goethe Plakette (Hone, 431 fn. 2), needed a prologue to "help the illusion and give the necessary atmosphere," as well as a more summary ending (Hone *Letters*, No. 101).

Cp. Yeats, Preface to various revised eds. of 7 (*v. Variorum*, 846-49), 86 (A, 336), "The Circus Animals' Desertion" (85, 86, or 88), and extract from speech at T. P. Gill's dinner (9 May 1899), copied in Reid, p. 93; Beerbohm, 1899 art.; Robinson, 49-54. V. also Yeats and Johnson in *Beltaine*, I (May 1899).

THE LAND OF HEART'S DESIRE

1: Correctly dated (for both earliest publication and earliest production) 1894.
2a: 4, 5: rev., 6, 7 (cp. Glossary note, 1901 ed.; some changes for 1912 rptg.), 30, 33a, 34, 43: rev., 44, 55 (text as in 5), 61 (with 10 Mar. 1923 "Preface" and bracketing of passages to be omitted in performance), 64, 66, 73, 78, 87 (best ed.).
 b: V. Wade *Biblio.*, 352, 353, 357, 360, 363, 369, 371.
 3: 29 Mar. 1894; Avenue Theatre, Northumberland Ave.,

London, then managed by Florence Farr (*v. infra*): a note in 5 says the play "ran for a little over six weeks." Miss A. E. F. Horniman helped finance this production (Robinson, *IAT*, 87). For original cast, history, and Yeats's changed regard for the play, *v.* its preface and "Note" in 61 (A, 301-2, 329) and cp. Hone, 114-15. This work was attacked as "a revolting burlesque of Irish Catholic religion" in F. H. O'Donnell's *The Stage Irishman of the Pseudo-Celtic Drama* (1904). Cp. Boyd, *CDI*, 62-63.—Not produced by Abbey until 16 Feb. 1911: for cast, *v.* Robinson, *IAT*, 105.

4: Written in response to Florence Farr's suggestion that Yeats provide a play in which to introduce Miss Farr's niece, Dorothy Paget, as a child actor, the play was begun by early Jan., finished by Feb., 1894 (Wade, 229, 195); within a decade (cp. *Idem*, 434) it was subjected to revision, Yeats having become dissatisfied with its "exaggeration of sentiment and sentimental beauty." It was again revised, early 1912 (*Idem*, 567), before the 22 Feb. production at the Abbey (cp. "Note," dated 1912, in 61).—On the names "Hart" and "Bruin" ("Mary Bruin" was "Maire Bruin" in the earlier editions), *v.* Wade, 908. (Yeats has a "Ballad of Father O'Hart": 85, 86, or 88.)

The final state of the play differs greatly from the pre-1912 versions; 87 agrees almost exactly with 61: there are only minor differences in spelling, punctuation, and one or two phrases. Incidentally, the parentheses in the stage directions on p. 39 of 87A—and there is a corresponding set in 87E—make no sense, since they enclose a reference to an action Yeats did not exclude from the suggested acting version.

5: *Gloss*:

P. 35, l. 16: Ocris Head: Probably Aughris Head, a promontory on Sligo Bay.

P. 40, l. 7: "a cloudy blossoming of hair": Cp. "The shadowy blossom of my hair" ("The Heart of the Woman") and "a cloud of her hair" ("The Cap and Bells"): 85, 86, or 88.

l. 11: "blessed quicken wood": Act I of an early version of *The Countess Cathleen* has "What, would you burn the blessed quicken wood? / A spell to ward off demons and ill faeries."—Quicken is mountain ash, to the ancient Irish one of the three sacred—and seven "chieftain"—trees.

l. 26: Cp. "The Lover Tells of the Rose in His Heart": 85, 86, or 88.

P. 41, l. 15: Coolaney: In north central Sligo.

P. 42, Child's first speech: Cp. "The Song of the Old Mother" (pub. in the *Bookman*, Apr. 1894): 85, 86, or 88.

Child's last speech: Cp. the Greek, in *The Resurrection*: "That makes me shudder. The utmost possible suffering as an object of worship!"

P. 44, l. 18: Ballygawley Hill: Ballygawley is a town in the southern part of Co. Tyrone.

P. 45, l. 7: Nuala: "Finvara and Nuala . . . the arch-king and queen of the fairy host of Connacht . . .": Hyde, *Beside the Fire*, 87.—Aengus: V. notes to preceding play.

l. 8: Fiachra: ?—V. "The Poet Pleads with the Elemental Powers," *Proleg. I*. There was a Ulidian named Fiacra who accompanied Fergus and the other warriors who left Conchubar's service for Medb's; one of the children of Ler was named Fiachra; and the fourth century Niall of the Nine Hostages had a brother named Fiachra.

l. 10: Finvara, "ruler of the Western Host": ". . . Western Faeries."—V. "Nuala," *supra;* cp. "Ethna the Bride" (Lady Wilde, 42-45).

ll. 11-12: Cp. the picture of the Land of the Young in "The Wanderings of Oisin," I.

P. 46, ll. 3-4: Cp. "The Hosting of the Sidhe" (85, 86, or 88).

l. 16: "White bird": Cp., for association, "The White Birds" (85, 86, or 88); according to Yeats's recollection, the birds of Faery were white. (*Proleg. I.*)

Reid, 100 ff., has interesting comment.

CATHLEEN NI HOULIHAN

1: Correctly dated (for both earliest publication and earliest production) 1902.

2a: *Samhain*, Oct. 1902, pp. 24-31 (with title hyphenated and surname spelled "Hoolihan"); 9 ("Hoolihan"), 16 ("Hoolihan"): rev., 17, 18, 24, 31, 33b, 41, 59, 73, 78, 87.—*N.B.* Lyrics separately published in *The United Irishman,* 5 May 1902.—Despite Boyd (150), somewhat, though not markedly, revised. Final version agrees almost exactly with that of 59.

b: V. Wade *Biblio.*, 351, 353, 355, 360, 363, 370.

3: 2 Apr. 1902; St. Teresa's Total Abstinence Association Hall, Clarendon St., Dublin; by W. G. Fay's "Irish National Dramatic Co.," with Maud Gonne appearing very effectively in the title role. For cast, *v.* Robinson, *IAT*, 27-31; reception, Wade, 368; heroine's part, *Idem*, 441, and Hone, 183-84; effect, M. Gonne, in *Scattering Branches* (ed. Gwynn), Gwynn, 158, Mc-Greevy, 24-25, and Robinson, *TH*, 218 (". . . *Kathleen ni Houlihan* and *The Rising of the Moon* have made more rebels in Ireland than a thousand political speeches or a hundred reasoned books").—Translated into Irish by Tomás Luibhéid for Abbey production of 20 Apr. 1946.

4: Yeats says this originated in a dream (*v.* 61: A, 56) and denies it was intended as propaganda (*Idem*, 160-61).—*Sinn Féin* for 25 Jan. 1913 makes the editorial claim (by Arthur Griffith?), Yeats "wrote at our suggestion the ending of Kathleen ni Houlihan as it is now played. . . ." (One trusts this does not imply an attempt to claim the final—and one really inspired—bit of dialogue!)—Cp. 59 (A, 426-28) or the prefatory dedication to 12; Lady Gregory, *OIT*, 82.—For the "Shan Van Vocht" ("The Poor Old Woman": i.e., Ireland), *v.* Brooke and Rolleston, *A Treasury of Irish Poetry*, 22; cp. Gwynn, 160.

5: *Gloss*:

"Cathleen ni Houlihan" is, of course, one of the numerous symbols for Ireland incarnate.

P. 50: Killala: In Co. Mayo: The French (*c.* 1,000

men) under Gen. Humbert landed there 22 Aug. 1798.—V. MacManus, 522.

P. 51, twelfth l. from bottom: Ballina: A town in northeastern Mayo, between Lake Conn and Killala Bay.

P. 52, l. 16: Enniscrone: ? Inchicronan (S of Tubber, in Co. Clare).

Bridget's third speech: "a poor scholar": Cp. Padraic Colum's "An Old Scholar of the Forties" (*Wild Earth*): a "hedge scholar." V. Saul, 43 fn. 10.

P. 53, last l.: "My four beautiful green fields": Metaphor for Ireland, the "strangers" of several lines earlier being the English.

P. 54, l. 2: Kilglass: A village E of Killala Bay.

Old Woman's fifth speech: O'Donnells: The reference is to the sixteenth-century Ulster prince "Red Hugh" O'Donnell: v. MacManus, 379 ff.— O'Sullivans: The reference is presumably to the sixteenth-century Donal O'Sullivan, of Dunboy Castle and Leitrim fame: v. MacManus, 394.— "Brian . . . Clontarf": King Brian Boru, slain during the rout of the Norse at Clontarf, Palm Sunday 1014.

P. 56, middle (3d l. of song): "the white-scarfed riders": Involves a reference to priestly habiliments at funerals (McGreevy, 25, fn. 2).

Malone (137) counts this "probably the most dramatically effective one-act play in Irish drama, as it is also one of the greatest one-act plays of the modern theatre."—Cp. Yeats's letter, "Mr. Yeats' New Play," *The United Irishman*, 5 Apr. 1902; notes, "The Acting at St. Teresa's Hall," *Do.*, 12 and 26 Apr. 1902; and "The Man and the Echo"

(85, 86, or 88).—Dillon (*Early Ir. Lit.*, 188) says Yeats (p. 54) uses the folk song *Donnchadh Bán* ("Flaxen-haired Donough").

THE POT OF BROTH

1: Dated in 87 for earliest *book* publication: note records below.

2a: *The Gael* (N.Y.), Sept. 1903; 16, 17, 18, 23, 59, 73, 78, 87.—87E has (1957) the best available version; it agrees with that of 73 except for the tramp's last song. Indeed, the differences between the earliest and latest versions of this play are not greatly significant except with respect to that considerably worked-over song.

b: V. Wade *Biblio.*, 355, 372.

3: 30 Oct. 1902; Antient Concert Rooms (*v. C. Cathleen*); by "Irish National Dramatic Co.," of which Yeats was president. For cast, *v.* Robinson, *IAT*, 31.— Cp. Lady Gregory, *OIT*, 83.

4: Apparently written by 7 Sept. 1902 (cp. Wade, 377), this was until within a couple of months of production called "The Beggarman" (the "Tramp" being initially "A Beggarman" in the list of characters).—

V. 59 (A, 428-30).—Boyd (*CDI*, 72) calls this play "obviously the work of Lady Gregory," and its general lack of quality might well argue as much.—On the transformation of a song from this play into the first of "Two Songs Rewritten for the Tune's Sake," *v. Proleg. I.*—"Jack the journeyman" reappears in Yeats's *Words for Music Perhaps.*—The essential theme of the play is a variant of that of the centuries-old story of stone, or St. Bernard's, soup: cp. *Brewer's Dictionary . . .*, 867.

5: *Gloss*:

P. 60, Tramp's second speech: "Fiannta-h-Eireann": The *fianna* (*fena*), a species of legendary professional infantry who supposedly spent half the year hunting and camping (cp. Saul, 91).—Tramp's third speech: Tubber: A village, SW Galway, border of Co. Clare.—"kippeens": hambones.

P. 63, Sibby's second speech: "Sidhe" (pron. "shee"): *síde*: the elf-folk; *v.* Saul, 18-19.—John's first speech: Limerick: Chief town, Co. Limerick; on estuary of R. Shannon.—Tramp's seventh speech: "Slanlus": lichen, or a healing herb.—Tramp's eighth speech: "Fearavan": creeping buttercup, or crowfoot.—Tramp's ninth speech: "Athair-talav": ground ivy.

P. 64, Tramp's fourth speech: Clare: Co. Clare; W coast county, N and W of the Shannon.

P. 65, l. 1: Lochlann: Norway.—Song: "Paistin Finn": "White, *or* Fair, Paistin"; cp. §4, *sup*.

P. 67, l. 5: Ennis: County town, and capital, of Co. Clare; on R. Fergus.

Though trivial, and apparently little valued by Yeats, this play is said to be surprisingly effective in production. Cp. Roberts, 637.

THE KING'S THRESHOLD

1: Correctly dated for earliest publication.

2a: 19, 20, 21, 25: new version, 30, 33, 40, 41, 44, 51; 56 has "A New End for 'The King's Threshold'" and a note; 59, 73, 77: text from 59, 87.—Best text available (1957): 87E, with that of 73 in only minor disagreement. Yeats's essential notes were abstracted from 25 for 59.—*N.B.* "A Prologue" was published in *The United Irishman,* 9 Sept. 1903; in 20; in Wade's first *Biblio.* (Stratford-on-Avon: Shakespeare Head Press, Nov. 1908, with a footnote by Yeats dated 1904); and in Vol. II of the 1908 *Collected Works* (*v.* 33).

b: V. Wade *Biblio.,* 360, 371.

3: 8 Oct. 1903; Molesworth Hall, Dublin; by "Irish National Theatre Society." For cast, *v.* Robinson, *IAT,* 33; or 59 (A, 432). Production financed by Miss A. E. F. Horniman, who, according to Yeats (61: A, 68), also "designed and made the costumes."—Cp. Lady Gregory, *OIT,* 83.

4: The first version was certainly ready by 8 Aug. 1903

(cp. Wade, 409). The play is spoken of by Yeats as "partly rewritten," 15 Feb. 1905 (*Idem*, 448), and as almost completely revised by 30 May 1905 (*Idem*, 449); rehearsals, however, led to many further changes. The work owes slightly to *Sancan the Bard* (1905), a play by Edwin Ellis based on a story provided by Yeats (*v*. 59: A, 25-26), and—somewhat remotely—to a Middle Irish tale from the satiric *Immtheacht na Tromdáimhe* (*v. Transactions of the Ossianic Society*, V. I, and Lady F. Wilde's *Ancient Legends . . . of Ireland . . .* : London, 1902; 159 ff.), in which Seanchan, the chief bard, having demanded a feast, desires out of annoyance with the guests to have the Connacht nobles dismissed; eventually satirizes mice (their breed having devoured the remnants of a meal he had desired) and the cats who had not killed them; and is humiliated by Irusan, the vengeful head cat. As Miss Hoare has pointed out (121), Yeats "has completely reversed the meaning of the situation," symbolizing "the conflict between worldly power and poetry, and the ultimate triumph of the poet" (*Idem*, 120): cp. 61 (A, 40).

The 1904 version (*v*. 20) prints an unused prologue by "An Old Man" which, amusingly, argues that an ending in which Seanchan does not die (of course he *does* in the final version) is the right ending; this version also makes demotion from the king's table the crux of the whole situation, provides two pupils ("Senias" and "Arias") and two servants ("Cian" and "Brian") for Seanchan, and names the princesses "Buan" and "Finnhua" and the court ladies "Aileen" and "Essa." The earlier versions of this much-reworked and much-recast play are shorter, less adroit and amusing in handling the Mayor, and in general less aptly phrased; they end with capitulation of the king and gracious triumph for Seanchan, who returns the surrendered crown. (Cp. 59: A, 432.)

5: *Gloss*:

P. 70: Gort: Village in Co. Galway, W of Slieve Aughty Mountains.

P. 71, ll. 15-20: Perhaps a strained probability is here implied if Irish tradition is sound anent regard for poets.

P. 72, Seanchan's speech: Almhuin: Site of Finn's great hall; *v.* notes to *C. Cathleen.* One may cp. Saul, IV, §3; "The Wanderings of Oisin" (85, 86, or 88); and *Proleg. I.*—Finn: Greatest leader of the *fianna.*—Osgar: Finn's grandson; Oisin's son. —Grania: Heroine, Diarmuid-Grania story. Cp. Saul, 102-3.

P. 73, l. 17: "school": In ancient and medieval Ireland, apprentice bards studied rigorously under masters, *filid* (in early times) or *baird* (in later): cp. Saul, 42-45.

P. 74, l. 6: "Men of Dea": The Dé Danann race: the people of the mother-goddess Dana (Ana, etc.): cp. Saul, 19-20.

l. 7: "four treasures": The Dagda Mor's cauldron of plenty; the *Lia Fail,* or "Stone of Destiny"; and the conquering sword and spear of Lugh: cp. Keating, I, 207-11, and *v.* Cross, F244.1.* (p. 250) for references.—"Grail King": Presumably Pelles, the "Fisher King" of Arthurian romance; grandfather of Galahad.

ll. 29-30: It is interesting to cp. George Russell's assertion (*Destructive Censorship,* pub.

1929): "I will believe in no prophet of the Lord unless his words, even in anger, break in a foam of beauty on the ear."

P. 75, ll. 6-10: Cp. l. 3, "Lapis Lazuli" (85, 86, or 88), and Yeats's concept of tragedy.—Stage direct.: "Ogham" (*ogam*): A sort of alphabetic engraving.

P. 76, l. 4: Inchy (<?Ir. *inis*: cp. Lat. *insula*: "island"): ? A reference to one of the "Seven Woods" of Coole.—"Inch" is a common Irish place-name.—Kiltartan: Village a few miles N of Gort, Co. Galway.—Mayor's sixth speech: Kinvara: Kinvarra: Village NW of Kiltartan, off an eastern bend of Galway Bay.

P. 77, 2d l. from bottom: Duras: ". . . beyond Kinvara and beside the sea" (Lady Gregory, *OIT*, 3).

P. 78, mid-page: St. Colman, "holy well": Cp. notes to *The Cat and the Moon*.

P. 80, l. 3: "get the clapper . . .": hush up.

P. 83, l. 1: "mouthfuls of sweet air": Cp. St. 2, closing song, *At the Hawk's Well;* "For what have we in this life but a mouthful of air?" (*John Sherman*); "I made it out of a mouthful of air" ("He Thinks of Those Who Have Spoken Evil of His Beloved": 85, 86, or 88, and *Proleg. I*); Ellmann, *Iden.*, 325.

l. 30: "whey-faced metal": Silver.

P. 85, l. 13: "not civil yet": not yet dead (cp. ll. 2-3, p. 83).

P. 86, l. 20: "he cannot have you at his table": the cause of Seanchan's fasting (and therefore the dramatic motivation) in the early versions of the play; later the motivation became exclusion from the royal council. Did Yeats slip here?—or does "table" imply "council table"?

P. 88, l. 10: "He": The moon.

P. 91, l. 24: "A broken shoe": Cp. Synge's later *Deirdre of the Sorrows*: "I have put away sorrow like a shoe that is worn out and muddy . . ." (Act III).

P. 93, l. 13: Yeats again refers to Ezekiel in "To a Young Beauty": cp. 85, 86, or 88, and *Proleg. I.*

P. 94, Youngest pupil's last speech: Attributed by Hone (197) to Yeats's reading of Nietzsche.

N.B. Seanchan's fasting unto death was entirely in line with ancient Irish tradition: cp. Saul, 24.—Miss Ellis-Fermor (92) sees here Yeats's "conception of the artist's function"—his "proclamation of the absolute value of poetry."—Cp. Beerbohm, 1904 art.; Higgins, in Robinson, *IT*, 78-79; Lady Gregory's *OIT*, 83, for a collaborator's claimed share. One may also cp. Reinert, though this "explication" may seem a luminous effort in absurdity; Block may also be considered, wisely with some caution. Colum (*Dial* and *Theatre Arts Monthly*) has interesting comment. For suggested political implications, *v.* McGreevy, who notes that Yeats's revision of the play was made after the hunger-strike martyrdom of Terence MacSwiney, Lord Mayor of Cork. McGreevy feels that the inappreciative response of Irish audiences to this play is due to loss of "contact with the poetic tradition in the theatre."

THE SHADOWY WATERS
(Acting Version)

N.B. V. 85, 86, or 88, and *Proleg. I* for reading version and preliminary poems.

1: Misdated in 87: the "acting version" was first published in 1907; 1911 dates inclusion in 41.

2a: Publication Record of *both* versions: *North American Rev.*, May 1900; 8, 25: rev., 26: Acting Version (with Lady Gregory), 30: both versions (as in 25 and 26), 33: both versions, 35: 1906 version of 25 with note as in 33, 41 and 44: both versions, 58: 1906 version, 59: Acting Version, 62-63 and 69 and 70: 1906 version, 73 and 78: Acting Version, 85 and 86: 1906 version, 87: Acting Version.—*N.B.* "Introduction to a Dramatic Poem" was published in *The Speaker*, 1 Dec. 1900, and untitled when used in 8.

b: V. Wade *Biblio.*, 353, 355, 356, 360, 363, 366, 369, 371.

3: *Original prod.*: 14 Jan. 1904; Molesworth Hall, Dublin; by "Irish National Theatre Society." For cast, *v.* Robinson, *IAT*, 41. Staged by Robert Gregory.
First prod., Special Acting Version: 8 Dec. 1906; Abbey Theatre, Dublin; by "National Theatre Society, Ltd." (Abbey Co.) For cast, *v.* 59 (A, 433).

4: Cp. Ellmann, 74, 131; Reid, on long genesis, 108-9.—The play was under way in Nov. 1894 (Wade, 236).

On its history through 26, *v., idem,* 237 fn. 4; 25 has
detailed "Notes" anent first production and reworking
(in verse) in anticipation of new production. Cp. also
Wade, 245, 279, 280, 320, 322, and 323 for passing
references to the play's progress; for amusing side-
lights, *v.* Moore, *H&F,* I, 250 ff. On 21 Dec. 1899,
Yeats wrote Lady Gregory it was substantially finished (Wade, 332); a letter to Frank Fay says, "It is
almost religious, it is more a ritual than a human
story. It is deliberately without human characters"
(*Idem,* 425). On 30 May 1905, Yeats says he has "just
completed the revision of *Shadowy Waters*" (*Idem,*
449); by 15 July 1905, he is again revising (*Idem,*
453—and cp. 454-55, 460, and 462 for revealing comment); in 1907 (*Idem,* 491) he writes of three versions.—V., too, Yeats's notes in 25 and *The Arrow,* 24
Nov. 1906, pp. 3-4; 61 (A, 68-69); 59 (A, 426 and
433).

5: *Gloss*:

> P. 98, l. 23—p. 99, l. 4: Una Ellis-Fermor (102)
> cps. "Solomon and the Witch" (*v.* 85, 86, or 88):
> "Maybe the bride-bed . . ."; and *Essays, 1931
> to 1936,* p. 130. In her phrasing, "in *The Shad-
> owy Waters* the central theme is realization of
> ideal love in terms of, not by the superseding of,
> natural love. . . ."

N.B. For detailed notes, *v. Proleg. I.*

Parkinson is concerned with the revisions of this play
in §2 of his essay. Sister M. Rosalie Ryan (22) feels "the
denouement lacks dramatic conviction" because Dectora
"has been won by magical means."—The version in 85, 86,
or 88 is, as undamaged by the Lady Gregory touch, much

to be preferred.—Professor Alspach is (1957) preparing for publication a unique version of this play from a Huntington Library MS.

DEIRDRE

1: Correctly dated for earliest publication.

2a: 29 + 29a ("Alterations"), 30, 33, 38: with slight textual revision, 41: with new note, 44, 46, 49, 59: rev., 73, 78, 87.—Best available text (1957): 87E; 59A is especially faulty.

b: V. Wade *Biblio.*, 360.

3: 24 Nov. 1906; Abbey Theatre; by "National Theatre Society, Ltd." (Abbey Co.)—For cast, *v.* Robinson, *IAT*, 79; cp. 59 (A, 433-34). Scenery designed and painted by Robert Gregory. On reception, *v.* Wade, 482.

4: This play—its source in Lady Gregory's *Cuchulain of Muirthemne* (59: A, 425), though its plot departs therefrom freely—was apparently long in developing, and there are almost no public records. Yeats apparently first did a prose version. An undated letter to Florence Farr, which I should personally place between 30 Sept. and 6 Oct. 1905, remarks, "I do believe I have made a great play out of Deirdre . . . most powerful and even sensational"; and a 30 Sept. 1905 letter to the same friend records that the twelve lines beginning "There's nothing here for tears" were written that morning. But he was obviously still at work on the verse in the autumn of 1906 (cp. Wade, 476, 479, 480) and presumably finished the work in Oct. (v., *Idem*, 482), having done it largely at Coole. —V. Yeats's 1 Dec. 1906 letter to Katharine Tynan (*The Middle Years*, 356-57), and his notes in *The Arrow*, 24 Nov. 1906, p. [2]. It was no blessing that Lady Gregory wrote "the end" of this mainly splendid play (v. Wellesley, 51).

5: *Gloss*:

P. 117, l. 3: "raddle": Here, rouge.

l. 10: "Surracha": ?—Could this = "Sorcha" (v. gloss to *On Baile's Strand*)?

P. 120, ll. 14-15: "Istian," "Fanes": ?

P. 121, ll. 26-27: A traditional epithet for Fergus Mac Roig was "Fergus Honeymouth."

P. 129, third l. from bottom: "King of Leodas": ?— an imaginary Pictish king?—the "Lord of Duntreon" (L. Gregory, 134)?

For the legendary versions of the famous Deirdre story, one of the *remscéla* of the epic *Táin Bó Cuálnge* ("Cattle-Raid of Cooley"), and for identification of characters, one may consult Saul, 70, 74-77. As usual, Yeats handles recorded legend with a free hand—e.g., in the First Musician's account of Deirdre's early history and in the method of Naoise's taking.

On the verse, cp. Sturge Moore (Hone, 225).—In *Samhain* for 1904 (cp. 33b, 143), Yeats had announced his intention to make the "choruses somewhat in the Greek manner"; this is approved by Gwynn, who (*Fort. Rev.*,

346) nevertheless feels the play lacks the Aristotelian "magnitude." Roberts (637) asserts, "any line has more depth and more beauty than can be found in any act of other dramatists"; and McGreevy (21) counts this play "more classical" and "more definitely of the theatre" than Synge's *Deirdre of the Sorrows*. Nevertheless, Colum (*Theatre Arts Mthly.*, 940) attacks this work as one in which not a single character "has real dignity."

Cp. Robinson, 56-60; Lady Gregory, *OIT*, 83.

AT THE HAWK'S WELL

1: Correctly dated for earliest publication.

2a: As "At the Hawk's Well or Waters of Immortality" (with a preface; cp. "Instead of a Theatre," Wade *Biblio.*, 333), *Harper's Bazar*, Mar. 1917, and (without pref.) *To-day* (London), June 1917; with title clipped for book publication, 52: with original "Note," 53: a curiosity of no critical significance, 56, 61, 73, 87.—Best available text (1957): 87E.—*N.B.* The concluding lyric was first printed as "The Well and the Tree" in 51.

b: No record.

3: 2 Apr. 1916; Lady Cunard's drawing room (Cavendish Square, London, house): details not publicized, though it is known that Edmund Dulac provided the masks and the Japanese Michio Ito did a dance for this imitation of Nō drama (cp. 61: A, 334; Suzuki; Thompson; Bottomley; Mills). On production excitements, initially and two days later, *v.* Wade, 610-12—and cp. 892.

4: According to Ellmann (212, and cp. foll. pp.), this was "dictated to Pound early in 1916"; it became one of the "Four Plays for Dancers," for which a general preface, music, and extensive notes may be found in 61.—Yeats calls the hawk "one of the natural symbols of subjectivity" (61: A, 472); he claimed this play introduced masks "in serious drama in the modern world" (Wade, 610) and made only very minor changes in it after the 56 version. The music and "Note . . ." (originally the preface in *Harper's Bazar*) from 56 were reprinted, the latter with slight changes, in 61.

5: *Gloss:*

P. 136, Song: Cp. third speech, Ghost of Cuchulain, p. 191.

P. 137, Song: "A mother . . .": Cp. St. V, "Among School Children" (85, 86, or 88).

P. 138, l. 32: "Sidhe": Cp. notes to *The Pot of Broth.*

P. 139, l. 15: "Sualtim's": More usually (and in the earliest printings of this), "Sualtam's."

P. 143: "Aoife" (*Aife*, etc.): The Amazon on whom Cuchulain begat Conlaech. V. Saul, 87.

P. 144, Song: "I am but a mouthful of sweet air": Cp. notes to *The King's Threshold.*

On the Irish hero and demigod Cuchulain (*Cu Chulainn*: "Hound of Culann"), and on associated characters and tales, one may cp. Saul, IV, C, 2, *passim.* There is no authority for the fable of this play in recorded legend. The play itself is, of course, logically placed first in Yeats's Cuchulain cycle (*v., inf., The Green Helmet, On Baile's Strand, The Only Jealousy of Emer,* and *The Death of Cuchulain*).

One recalls William Morris' *The Well at the World's End* and the folk tale "The Well of D'Yerree-in-Dowan" (Hyde's *Beside the Fire*).—Cp. Yeats's letter of 1 Jan. 1898 to Dorothea Hunter (Wade, 293); and Ure (20), who feels "unity of being" is "represented by the plashing water in the well." Gogarty (245) says Yeats called the well "The well of immortality or of wisdom" and referred to the hawk-woman as "intellect." McGreevy (31) asserts, "The Guardian represents the forces that draw man away from everything that transcends the mediocre and the every-day."

THE GREEN HELMET / AN HEROIC FARCE

1: Correctly dated (for both earliest publication and earliest production) 1910.

2a: Prose *The Golden Helmet* (32, 33b) > verse *The Green Helmet*: 36, 37; *Forum*, Sept. 1911; 39, 41: with new note, 45, 59, 73, 78, 87.—Best available text

(1957), 87E, though, except for many changes in punctuation and a few minor touches, the different versions of *The Green Helmet* are remarkably close to textual agreement.

b: Trans. of *The Golden Helmet*: v. Wade *Biblio.*, 360.

3: *The Golden Helmet*: 19 Mar. 1908; Abbey Theatre; "National Theatre Society, Ltd." (Abbey Co.)—For cast, v. Robinson, *IAT*, 81.

The Green Helmet: 10 Feb. 1910; Abbey prod. as above.—For cast, v. Robinson, *op. cit.*, 103; on production desiderata, v. 59 (A, 436-37).

4: The verse version was apparently in large degree finished by 8 Mar. 1909 (cp. Wade, 525), though to the point of possible publication perhaps only by the beginning of the next year (*Idem*, 545-46).—Yeats says it is founded on "The Feast of Bricriu" (*Cuchulain of Muirthemne*) and intended as an introduction to *On Baile's Strand* (59: A, 425). One should cp. also an allied tale, *The Bargain of the Strong Man* ("The Championship of Ulster" in its *Cuchulain of Muirthemne* guise). As usual, Yeats employs a very free hand with his source material.—Cp. the fourteenth-century Middle English *Sir Gawayne and the Grene Knight*.

5: *Gloss*:

P. 148, l. 2: Connacht—*Connachta*, its capital Cruachan (modern Rathcroghan, Co. Roscommon: cp. Keating, II, 187 ff.)—was one of the five ancient Irish kingdoms ("fifths"), in Cuchulain's day ruled over by Oilioll (Ailill) and his warlike, amorous queen, Medb.

P. 150, ll. 19-20: A reference to the story of King Ruad (*Book of Ballymote*).

P. 151, l. 3: "rath": an elf-mound, or fort.

P. 152, l. 18: Manannan: sea-god, son of Ler.

l. 19: "Red Man of the Boyne": ?—Could this be Ross the Red, son-in-law of Aengus Mac-in-Og?—Padraic Colum, in a personal letter, suggests "just a supernatural being—Fear Darrig."

l. 26: "Sualtim's son": V. notes to *At the Hawk's Well*.

Laegaire (Loegaire) "the Triumphant" and Conall Caernach ("the Victorious") are two of the leading heroes of the Ulster, or Red Branch, Cycle of Irish tales; Conall (*The Red Rout of Conall Caernach*: v. Saul, 85-86) was eventually the avenger of Cuchulain.—On Emer, one may also cp. Saul (86-87).

Though a good play, *The Golden Helmet* is less vitally poetic and less exciting than *The Green Helmet*: by comparison, more suggestive of a polished scenario than of a play. Its conclusion, too, is more prosaic in motivation (Cuchulain offers his head to secure promised "peace" for Ireland) than that of the verse derivative, which has consequently greater tension—and which also gives Emer a richer part. The last speech of *The Golden Helmet* may be quoted as suggestive of a touchstone of comparative quality:

I will not harm you, Cuchulain. I am the guardian of this land, and age after age I come up out of the sea to try the men of Ireland. I give you the championship because you are without fear, and you shall win many battles with laughing lips and endure wounding and betrayal without bitterness of heart; and when men gaze upon you, their hearts shall grow greater and their minds clear; until the day come

when I darken your mind, that there may be an end
to the story, and a song on the harp-string.

Boyd (162-63) remarks the initial injection by Yeats of
humor into a heroic theme. Cp. Colum's sound approval,
Theatre Arts Mthly., 941-42.

ON BAILE'S STRAND

N.B. Cp. "Cuchulain's Fight with the Sea" (85, 86, or 88)
and *Proleg. I.*

1: Misdated in 87: original version first published 1903;
   revised, 1906.

2a: 13, 14, 20, 22, 25: new version (*v.* Wade, 465; *Sha-
    nachie*, Spring 1906, for some fresh verses), 28, 30,
    33, 41, 44, 46, 59, 73, 78, 87.—Best available text
    (1957), 87E.—The final text is essentially established
    by the 1906 version (25); the earlier versions are
    vastly different for over half of the play, initially re-
    hearsing much legend and making clear that Con-
    cobar has come with other kings to Muirthemne to
    consult with Cuchulain over plans for rebuilding
    Emain (burnt after the Deirdre-Naoise tragedy),
    being generally more diffuse, and lacking the motiva-
    tion of Concobar's forcing Cuchulain to become his
    man, partly through worry over the succession. The

1906 and later versions, which differ among themselves in punctuation and a few verbal changes, are more compact and dramatic. As usual in the case of Yeats's revisions, they show that scarcely a line of sound poetry has been lost, though many lines have been improved. Incidentally, 25 has an interesting note, of which some matter was abstracted for 59: what was not abstracted is Yeats's plan for a cycle of Cuchulain plays.—Pre-1906 *dramatis personae* were listed as follows (cp. 20):

Cuchullain, the King of Muirthemne.
Concobar, the High King of Ullad.
Daire, a King.
Fintain, a blind man.
Barach, a fool.
A Young Man.
Young Kings and Old Kings.

b: V. Wade *Biblio.*, 355, 360, 371.

3: 27 Dec. 1904; Abbey Theatre (opening bill); by "Irish National Theatre Society." For cast, *v.* Robinson, *IAT*, 46; or 58 (A: 432-33). Staged by Robert Gregory.—For father's critical comment, *v.* Hone, 217-18. Pollock (37) has a vivid recollection.

4: This play is based by profession (58: A, 425) on "The Only Son of Aoife" (*Cuchulain of Muirthemne*: 1902); but Yeats wrote Griffith he was "just starting" it (originally referring to it as "Cuchullain") 16 July 1901 (Wade, 353), though he was apparently still working on it when *Kathleen ni Hoolihan* was produced. A note in 13 and 14 says he "thought out" much of the play while "walking about among the Seven Woods [of Coole]." (For the original Irish story, assigned to the ninth century by Meyer, *v.*

Ériu, I, 113.) The first version may have been essentially finished by 5 April 1902 (cp. Wade, 369), though Yeats was still revising passages in 1903 in preparation for publication in 13. By 20 Jan. 1904 he had seemingly done more reworking (on this and his concept of Cuchulain at that time, *v.*, *Idem*, 424-25); just before production, he named it his "best play" (*Idem*, 444); after performance, he rewrote it (*Idem*, 448), in preparation for 25. Some thirty years after production, he wrote Dorothy Wellesley (*Idem*, 913): " 'Cuchulain' seemed to me a heroic figure because he was creative joy separated from fear." (Cp., *sup.*, the quoted conclusion of *The Golden Helmet*. Suss argues this conception in a pontifical and unsympathetic article.)

5: *Gloss*:

P. 162, Dundealgan: Cuchulain's seat in Muirthemne (Dundalk area, Co. Louth).

P. 162, next-to-last l.: Boann: Minor divinity for whom the River Boyne was named; cp. *Cuchulain of Muirthemne*, 28-29.—Fand: Wife of the sea-god Manannan Mac Lir.

P. 164, Blind Man's second speech: "A young man": Conlaech, Cuchulain's son by the Hebrides Amazon Aoife; cp. Saul, 86, 87.—Fool's song: "Banachas and Bonachas": ? *bannanach* and *boccanach*: "white-faced" and "puck-faced" goblins, or sprites, respectively. Cp. Cross, F251.7.* (p. 251.)

P. 166, desc. of Cuchulain: Though Cuchulain is here said to be "something over forty years of age," tradition usually says he was slain at twenty-seven.

P. 167, l. 9: Maeve: *V.* notes to *The Green Helmet.*—"the northern pirates": The Norse marauders.

ll. 10-11: "kings of Sorcha . . .": Sorcha (*Sorca*) is part of the Celtic Otherworld; in *The Pursuit of the Giolla Decair,* Finn aids its king against the "King of the World," and Cuchulain (*Cuchulain of Muirthemne,* 217) is said to have had a cloak from "the King of Sorcha." As curiosities of reference, the stories in Macalister may here be recalled.

l. 15: I.e., "Am I an old man?"

l. 32: By implication, Cuchulain is here referred to as the son of Lugh, god of light—one of varying traditions. Cp. Saul, 21-22, 72-73.

l. 39: "a burning cloud": Cp. "Fallen Majesty" (85, 86, or 88), where the figure becomes a metaphor for Maud Gonne.

P. 169, l. 6: "Country-under-Wave": *V.* notes to *C. Cathleen.*

l. 11: "there was one": Aoife: *v. sup.*

P. 171, l. 13: "all's changed": Phrase recurs in St. 3 of "The Wild Swans at Coole" (85, 86, or 88).

l. 15: Druidic oath implied.

P. 172, l. 7: "them" = "themselves."

P. 173, l. 22: "to no man": More accurately, according to tradition, *to no unaccompanied inquirer;* however, Yeats follows Lady Gregory here (*Cuchulain of Muirthemne,* 314).

P. 174, l. 21: Cp. " 'The dooms of men are in God's hidden place.' " (*Cuchulain's Fight with the Sea.*)

l. 24: "he": Lugh.

P. 176, ll. 9-10: Cp. " 'Your head a while seemed
like a woman's head / That I loved once.' "
(*Cuchulain's Fight* . . .)

P. 180, middle (Cu's sixth speech): Scathach
("Shadowy"): The Amazon of Skye who taught
the young Cuchulain arms. Uathach, her daughter, was one of Cu's lovers.—"Alba" is Scotland.

P. 181, l. 10: Dubthach: "Dubtach Chafertongue":
In one tradition, one of Conchubar's emissaries
sent with Fergus to recall Deirdre and the Sons
of Usna from Scotland, and a deserter to Medb
after Conchubar's treachery.

l. 12: Laegaire: *V.* notes to *The Green Helmet.*

Cp. Ure and Bjersby, *passim*; Robinson, 60-63. For
Yeats's own analysis of Cuchulain and Conchubar, *v.*
Wade, 424-25; cp. 72 (A, 92-93) and "The Circus Animals' Desertion," II (85, 86, or 88). Gwynn (*Fort Rev.*,
343) feels that Yeats fails in "natural, convincing, trans-
missible emotion" when Cuchulain discovers whom he
has slain ("He was my son . . ."). Colum is sure the characters lack "heroic stature" (*Theatre Arts Mthly.*, 941).

THE ONLY JEALOUSY
OF EMER

1: Correctly dated for earliest publication.

2a: *Poetry* (Chicago), Jan. 1919; 54, 56, 61, 73, 87.—Satisfactory texts in 73 and 87. *N.B.* Out of this grew the triviality *Fighting the Waves* (72—dictated at Cannes: Wade, 753), the "Introduction" to which was originally published in the *Dublin Mag.*, Apr.-June 1932. *Fighting the Waves* saw initial production 13 Aug. 1929 at the Abbey Theatre; Antheil's music is printed in 72. The cast may be found in Robinson, *IAT*, 143. On the success of the production, cp. Wade, 767-68. *V.* also Robinson's *Curtain Up*, 68-69.

b: No record.

3: ? 1916 (Ellis-Fermor, 116); Mrs. Bjersby says the first public performance took place in Holland. Cp. Yeats's intro. in 72.

4: Yeats was pondering this play early in Apr. 1916 (Wade, 612); he finished it at Oxford on 14 Jan. 1918 (cp. *Idem*, 639, 645). The original preface to 54 was dated 11 Oct. 1918.—Cp., *supra*, At the Hawk's Well.

Ure (21) derives this (doubtless in line with Yeats's intention, though the connection is worse than tenuous) from the legendary Cuchulain-Fand story (*The Sickbed of Cuchulain*—behind Lady Gregory's "The

Only Jealousy of Emer," *Cuchulain of Muirthemne;*
v. Saul, 68); he calls it "a strange drama of conflict . . . between human love and the abstraction of
death. . . ."—Yeats's note in 61 is slightly revised from
that in 56.

Numerous small revisions are apparent in 56, with
which 61 is in practically absolute textual agreement;
major revisions are incorporated in 73, with which 87
agrees. The big change in the final version results
from Emer's resigning Cuchulain's love before the
hero awakes and reclaims Eithne Inguba; the earlier
versions come to a more confusing and less lucidly
presented conclusion.—Ellmann (230) feels Eithne
Inguba was "inspired by Iseult Gonne" (Maud's
adopted daughter).

5: *Gloss:*

P. 184, ll. 7 ff.: "How many centuries spent . . .":
Cp. "The Phases of the Moon" (85, 86, or 88: "All
dreams of the soul . . .").

l. 12: Archimedes: Greek mathematician of
3d century B.C.

P. 186, next-to-last l.: Manannan: *V.* gloss to *The
Green Helmet.*

P. 187, ll. 1-3: Cp. conclusion to "The Cold Heaven"
(85, 86, or 88) and *Proleg. I.*

P. 188, l. 28: "not the man": *I.e.,* not Concobar's
bitter poet (Saul, 70, 88).

P. 190, l. 14: "Country-under-Wave": *V.* notes to
C. Cathleen.

l. 16: "Sidhe": *V.* notes to *The Pot of Broth.*

l. 26: "cloudy hair": Cp. "a cloud of her
hair" ("The Cap and Bells": 85, 86, or 88).

P. 191, Ghost of Cuchulain's third speech: Cp. *At*

the Hawk's Well, p. 136. The reference is to the
guardian of the well; yet Bricriu, at the bottom
of p. 192, refers to the Woman of the Sidhe as
Fand, Manannan's wife.—Ghost of Cuchulain's
fourth speech: Cp. fifteenth phase of *A Vision*.

P. 194: The next-to-last stanza seems also to con-
note Yeats's "circuits of the moon" (*A Vision*).

THE HOUR-GLASS

1: The mixed (or so-called "verse") version included in
87 is there dated for earliest *book* publication; it had
periodical publication in 1913. (To some, the out-
and-out prose version will seem preferable: cp. Robinson, 63; not, however, to Colum: *Theatre Arts Mthly.*,
938-39.)

2a: As "The Hour-Glass. A Morality," *No. Amer. Rev.*,
Sept. 1903; oddly, the 1903 pamphlet edition (15),
which supposedly postdated the magazine printing,
was dated 29 Aug. by the British Museum (*v.* Wade
Biblio., It. 51). There followed 16, 17, 18, 27, 31, 33b,
and 41 (with a new Note). In Apr. 1913, Yeats published "The Hour Glass / *With a Preface to the New
Version*" in *The Mask* (Florence); the new version
of the play proper (partly verse, partly prose) first

appeared in book form in 47, which was followed by 48 (wherein the hyphen reappears), 51, 59: both versions, 73, 78, and 87.—87E offers (1957) the most satisfactory text; the almost-confusing evolution of the "new version" followed drastic revision of the *No. Amer. Rev.* text, as well as subsequent changes.

b: V. Wade *Biblio.*, 355, 360, 363, 369, 372.

3: *Prose Version*: 14 Mar. 1903; Molesworth Hall, Dublin; by "Irish National Theatre Society." For cast, *v.* Robinson, *IAT*, 33. (One notes Padraic Colum's appearance as a "pupil.")—Costumes designed by Robert Gregory (Lady Gregory, *OIT*, 107). Cp. Gwynn, 161.

"Verse" Version: 21 Nov. 1912; Abbey Theatre; Abbey Co.—Cp. 59 (A, 437).—Gordon Craig designed the costumes and screens for this production.

4: On the source of this play, *v.* 59 (A, 426), and cp. also, *Idem*, 430. V. "App. I" to 33b for a convenient reprint of Lady Wilde's story, in which the teacher (a priest who has gone against his religion and taken a wife, though he is not said to have children), allowed to choose a span of twenty-four hours to find a believer, is finally saved by the appearance of a believing child "'from a far country'" whom he instructs to murder him and call the pupils to watch the escaping soul (which becomes the "first butterfly that was ever seen in Ireland"). There is, incidentally, no prototype for Teigue.

Yeats at first referred to this play as *The Fool and the Wise Man* (Wade, 375). The first draft was "almost finished" by 13 June 1902 (*Idem*: a record contradicting Frank Fay in *Scattering Branches*, ed. Gwynn, 129), and the MS was ready for reading by

Dec. (*Idem*, 389.) It also appears that Yeats was planning verse transformation as early as Jan. 1903 (*Idem*, 391). Revision was in process early in 1912 (*Idem*, 567), but apparently not finished until 1913 (*Idem*, 393 fn.).—The early version seems the closer to the folk tale source, but Boyd (*CDI*, 74) argues the superiority of the later, in which the dead teacher's soul gets revised handling and certain passages have—though with no real dramatic gain—been put into Latin by Alan Porter.—Incidentally, the Angel got purely masculine reference in the *No. Amer. Rev.* and mainly masculine reference in 16, a sexual change being implied in the final stage directions of the latter!

5: *Gloss*:

> P. 197, Stage directions: "books": An obvious error for "book" (cp. opening directions and 59).— First Pupil's second speech: Cp. Yeats's 1924 footnote to "Anima Mundi," *Essays*, 523.—*Diem noctemque contendo, sed quos elegi, quos amavi, in tirocinium vel hi labuntur:* I argue day and night, but these whom I have chosen, whom I have loved, are being brought to trial.

> P. 198: *Virgas ut partus educant colligunt aves, mens hominis nugas:* The birds bind twigs together that they may nurture the young, the mind of man gathers trifles.

> P. 199, Fool's second speech: Tubber-vanach & Carrick-orus: *V.* notes to *C. Cathleen.*—Kilcluan: ?—Perhaps an invented name: "Church of the Meadow."

> P. 203, l. 1: "Fisher's": God's.

P. 204: W. M.: *Nullum esse deum dixi nullam dei matrem: mentitus vero: nam recte intelligenti sunt et deus et dei mater:* I have asserted God and the Mother of God to be nothing: but I have lied: both God and the Mother of God exist for the truly wise man.

F. P.: *Argumentis igitur proba; nam argumenta poscit qui rationis est particeps:* Now prove by arguments; for he who is a companion of reason demands arguments.

W. M.: *Pro certo habeo e vobis unum quidem in fide perstitisse, unum altius quam me vidisse:* I know for certain that one of you has remained firm in his faith, that one has seen higher than I.

W. M.: *Quae destruxi necesse est omnia reaedificem:* It is necessary that all I have destroyed be rebuilt.

F. P.: *Haec rationibus nondum natis opinabamur: nunc vero adolevimus: exuimus incunabula:* These things did not enter our childish minds: but now we have grown up: we have laid aside swaddling clothes.

F. P.: *Non iam pueri sumus; corpus tantummodo ex matre fictum est:* We are not now boys; only the body is conceived from the mother.

S. P.: *Docuisti; et nobis persuadetur:* You have taught; and we are convinced.

W. M.: *Mendaciis vos imbui, mentisque simulacris:* I have filled you with lies, and your minds with shadows.

S. P.: *Nulli non persuasisti:* You have persuaded no one.

Other Pupils: *Nulli, nulli, nulli:* No one. . . .

P. 205, S. P.: *Argumentum, domine, profer:* Produce the proof, O teacher.

P. 206, W. M.: *Credo in patrem et filium et spiritum sanctum:* I believe in the Father, the Son, and the Holy Spirit.

last l.: "sweet-throated things": Presumably angelic creatures.

P. 210, Wise Man's fifth speech: Hone (273) finds here the theme of *Where There Is Nothing*. Una Ellis-Fermor (98), commenting on the parallel passages in the prose version, cps. *Per Amica . . . ,* 24, and *Peer Gynt,* Act V.

P. 211, Wise Man's speech, ll. 6-8: Cp. Dante (Canto III, "Paradise," Cary trans. of the *Vision* [N.Y.: Hurst, n.d.], l. 6, p. 437): "And in his will is our tranquillity."

Miss Ellis-Fermor (108-9) points also to kinship with *Everyman;* Malone (137) calls this "the greatest morality play of the contemporary theatre." Cp. Frank Fay's emphatic endorsement (*op. cit., sup.*). Dume recalls in his dissertation that Yeats once referred to this play as "a parable of the conscious and the subconscious life"; cp. 61 (A, 47-48, 69, 129) and Henn, 263-66.

THE UNICORN FROM THE STARS

1: Correctly dated for earliest publication.

2a: *Where There Is Nothing*, published as a supplement to *The United Irishman*, 1 Nov. 1902 (cp. Wade *Biblio.*, It. 41), and as 10, 11, and 12 > *The Unicorn from the Stars*: 31, 33a, 59, 73, 87.—87E is (1957) by far the best available text.

b: *V.* Wade *Biblio.*, 357, 360, 372.

3: *Where There Is Nothing*: 26 June 1904; Royal Court Theatre, London; by London Stage Society, under the direction of Granville Barker. (On early preliminary plans, *v.* Wade, 385-86.)
The Unicorn . . . : 21 Nov. 1907; Abbey Theatre, Dublin; by "National Theatre Society, Ltd." (Abbey Co.) For cast, *v.* Robinson, *IAT*, 80.

4: *Where* . . . was written in 1902 by Yeats, Lady Gregory, and Douglas Hyde; perhaps finished in Sept. (Cp. Wade, 379, 503; on the construction of the play, *Idem*, 405-6. On the quarrel with George Moore over the rights to the plot, *v. Auto.*, 274-76; Jeffares, 10; Hone, 192-93.) On the transformation into *The Unicorn* . . . , mainly by Lady Gregory, one may consult 59 (A, 434-35); Yeats was apparently working on this in early summer of 1907 (cp. Wade, 483-84)—had seemingly not decided on the new title by mid-Sept. (*Idem*, 492.)—To his sister Elizabeth, he (*Idem*, 662) admitted the unicorn was a symbol from his "mystical order" and was "the soul"; he thought (*Idem*, 503) of the reworked play as carrying "to a more complete realization the central idea of the stories in *The Secret Rose*."

5: *Gloss*:

> *Passim*: Johnny Bocach: As late as 59, "Bacach": Ir. *bacac* ("lame man"), a rascally type of early nineteenth-century beggar.
>
> P. 217, Andrew's first speech: Kinvara: V. notes to *The King's Threshold*.
>
> P. 220: *Et calix meus inebrians quam praeclarus est*: And how splendid is the cup of my drunkenness.
>
> P. 227, Father John's third speech: St. Ciaran: Sixth-century founder of the school at Clonmacnois (Hyde, 204 ff.).
>
> P. 229, l. 7: "the day of the recognition of tricks": Judgment Day.—First stage directions: Should not "Nanny" logically be "Biddy" here, in view of Nanny's next speech?—Song, l. 1: "airy": ? carefree; last st.: Connotes deportation to felons' colony in Tasmania.
>
> P. 231, Biddy's first speech: Obviously a reference to groups given to civil disturbance: e.g., the "Peep o' Day" lads were violent Protestants who, about the break of the nineteenth century, would raid Catholic homes at daybreak looking for arms. Lady Gregory (*OIT*, 62) has a reference to "Whiteboys."

Paudeen's second speech: Columcille (*Colum Cille:* "Dove of the Church"), or Columba: Sixth-century prince and missionary to Britain. V. Hyde, Ch. XV.

P. 233, Johnny's second speech: "Seaghan Calvin's": John Calvin's.

P. 234: How could Martin give Paudeen the banner if all the beggars were sent to another room on p. 233?

P. 235, song: Foretells the triumph of Ireland over England.

P. 238: "Three that are watching . . .": An old Irish *rann.*

P. 239, l. 1: Aughanish: A headland on the Galway coast.

P. 244, Biddy's second speech: "Golden Plough": ?

P. 246, Martin: "The Mountain of Abiegnos": "For the members of the Golden Dawn [a secret society to which Yeats once belonged] . . . the Mountain of Abiegnos was the mountain of spiritual struggle, to be ascended only by those who had sufficiently purified themselves." (Ellmann, 188.)

In *The United Irishman,* 1 Nov. 1902, Yeats calls *Where . . .* a "picture of the soul of man." Cp. his piece of the same title in *The Secret Rose;* Ellmann, 132-33; Weygandt, 52-53; *Academy,* LXIII (n.s. 1597), 661-62.

Where . . . has a large cast, with seventeen named characters *et al.* Paul Ruttledge gives up his wealth seeking the "regeneration" of his soul—first by joining tinkers and becoming "the beggarman of all the ages" seeking the "wild beast, Laughter"; later by functioning as a visionary monk until his dismissal for preaching "We must de-

stroy the World; we must destroy everything that has
Law and Number, for where there is nothing, there is
God." Accused of witchcraft, he is eventually slain by the
risen populace.—This five-act affair, overburdened by
too much talk, is loose and vague in development. (Incidentally, Tommy the Song sings bits of "Down by the
Salley Gardens" in Act II.) Hone (273) sees its theme as
the "Perish . . . into reality" of *The Hour-Glass;* Boyd has
comment (*CDI*, 67 ff.). Miss Ellis-Fermor (104-7) offers
perceptive comparative observations on this play and *The
Unicorn* . . . (on the title of which, *v.* Tindall, 256; Moore,
Ch. VI).

THE PLAYER QUEEN

N.B. V. 85, 86, or 88, and *Proleg. I* on the lyrics "A Song
from 'The Player Queen,'" "The Mask," and the second
of "Two Songs Rewritten for the Tune's Sake."
 1: Correctly dated for earliest publication.
 2a: *The Dial,* Nov. 1922; 59, 60, 73, 87.—All major revi-
    sions of this play have to do with Sc. II, which was
    extensively reworked from the *Dial* version for 59 and
    60 (which are textually in agreement and have a
    "Note" on the genesis of the play), and from these
    for 73, where the play assumes final form (leaving

the question of whether its previous ending was not more appropriate to farce). 87E is (1957) the best available text.

b: V. Wade *Biblio.*, 357, 370, 372.

3: 25 May 1919; King's Hall, Covent Garden, London; by London Stage Society. [Abbey Theatre: 9 Dec. 1919; cast in Robinson, *IAT*, 130.]

4: On the evolution of this play, one may consult Yeats's introduction to "The Resurrection," 72: A, 93, and his note in 59 (A, 437-38), telling how it veered into farce from an intended verse tragedy illustrating certain aspects of what later became his "system" (*A Vision*). ("1907" in this note should presumably be "1908": cp. Wade, 511.) For an extract from an early draft, one may v. Ellmann, 168 (and cp. 183).—The scenario was begun ? Sept. 1908 (Wade, *Idem*); one prose draft was finished by Oct. (*Idem*, 512), with a verse version intended. Yeats tells his father he is "working at" the play, 27 Dec. 1908 (*Idem*, 513), but it is still a prose scenario on 8 Mar. 1909 (*Idem*, 525) . . . and "still all scenario" 17 July ?1909 (*Idem*, 532). On 12 Sept. 1914, Yeats tells his father it is "almost finished" (*Idem*, 588). On 11 May 1916 he is still retouching it (*Idem*, 614); about a year later he has just revised it (*Idem*, 625-26). (Cp. Ellmann, 167-73, 161 ff.)—On the amusing effort to win the interest of Mrs. Patrick Campbell (on whom Becker, quoting Mrs. Yeats as his authority, says Decima was modeled), v. Hone, 249; on the difficulties of writing Sc. II, v. Wade, 658. A 1 Dec. 1922 letter to Dulac (Wade, 693) suggests this play is one form of a "refuge from logic . . . passion . . . love of God . . . charity to my neighbours and other exhausting things."

5: *Gloss*:

P. 249: Anent Septimus' drunken condition, Hone (271) recalls "I see the blessedest soul in the world / And he nods a drunken head." ("The Blessed": 85, 86, or 88.)

P. 250, l. 5: Kubla Khan: Kublai Khan: thirteenth-century founder, Mongol dynasty, China.

5th l. from bottom: "Venus and Adonis . . .": A drunken confusion of Greek legend with astronomy.

P. 252, l. 2: Cp. Exodus 22:18.

P. 254, 5th l. from bottom: Candlemas: Celebrated 2 February.

P. 255, First Countryman's second speech: Cp. Matthew 21.

P. 257, l. 2: " 'The Tragical History of Noah's Deluge' ": ? A reference to the Chester miracle play *Noah and the Flood*.

last l.: "Old Man in the Sky": God: cp. "old man in the skies," "The Wild Old Wicked Man" (85, 86, or 88).

P. 258, Queen's first speech: "Holy Saint Octema": An invention.

10th l. from bottom: "eagle look": Recalls a favorite concept in Yeats's lyrics; cp., e.g., "Friends" or "His Phoenix."

6th l. from bottom: "Sleep of Adam!"—V. Genesis 2:21.

P. 260, l. 6: "all summer in a look": Cp. l. 12, "The Folly of Being Comforted" (85, 86, or 88).

P. 262, song, mid-page: Altered, but perhaps not improved, into a three-stanza piece as the second

of "Two Songs Rewritten for the Tune's Sake"
(*A Full Moon in March*).

P. 264, song: "Queen Pasiphae": Mother of the
Minotaur in Greek mythology.—"Queen Leda":
Cp. "Leda and the Swan" and "Lullaby" (85, 86,
or 88) and *Proleg. I.*

P. 265, third and fourth ll. from bottom: (M. Porcius) Cato, Cicero, Demosthenes: famous ancient
orators—first two Roman, last Greek; "Petronius
Arbiter . . .": cp. "Upon a Dying Lady," I (85,
86, or 88).

P. 266, "Xanadu" (Second Player's first speech): V.
Coleridge's *Kubla Khan;* "The Fall of Troy":
presumably an invented title.

P. 267, l. 5: "the Great Bear": Constellation Ursa
Major.—Septimus' third speech: "Man is nothing
till he is united to an image": Cp. Yeats's doc-
trine of the mask and the antiself; Ellmann,
Iden., 108-9.—Septimus' fourth speech: "Ionian . . .
Dorian": V. Ferguson, 15, 22, 29.

P. 268, fourth l. from bottom: Delphi: V. notes to
King Oedipus, inf.

P. 270, Old Beggar's fourth speech: Cp. Rossi's comment on Yeats's attitude toward the supernatural.

Though this is the play conceivably the most revelatory
of the mature Yeats, cp. Malone's astonishing opinion and
Robinson's surprising reservations (63-65). O'Connor is
perhaps more clear-sighted; cp. Jeffares (18), McGreevy
(34), Colum (*Theatre Arts Mthly.*, 942), and Becker
(though here the argument may be pressed too hard).—
On the play's tremendous effectiveness in a capable production, *v.* Roberts (636).

THE DREAMING OF THE BONES

1: Correctly dated for earliest publication.

2a: *The Little Review*, Jan. 1919; 54, 56, 61, 73, 87.—Except in spelling of proper names and punctuation, one of the least-revised of Yeats's plays. The *Little Rev.* text is the sorriest, both because the first and because the typesetting on that periodical left much to be desired; 73 and 87E are (1957) the best of the revised texts, and these do not differ importantly from 56 and 61.

b: No record.

3: ?1917. [Abbey Theatre production, 6 Dec. 1931: cast in Robinson, *IAT*, 146. On reception, *v*. Wade, 788.—Revival, 29 Nov. 1948, in Abbey's "Experimental Theatre": *v*. Robinson, *op. cit.*, 213, for cast.]

4: *V. At the Hawk's Well, supra*.—This play was completed in London (Hone, 324). One deduces from a 15 May 1917 letter that it had been "started" by then; an 11 June 1917 letter (Wade, 626) calls it "almost finished"; one of 12 August 1917 tells Lady Gregory it is finished (*Idem*, 629); and Rummel's music for the play (61: A, 442) is dated 1917. The preface to 54 is dated 11 Oct. 1918.—W. A. Henderson (cp. "Preface" to 56) furnished Yeats the "historical allusions to 'Dervorgilla.'"

5: *Gloss*:

P. 277, l. 4: Corcomroe: Ruined abbey, northern corner of Co. Clare, just across the border from Galway.

l. 12: Aran: The three Aran Islands are in the Atlantic, about thirty miles off the coast of Co. Galway.

l. 13: bawneen: < Ir. *bawn*: a walled cattle enclosure; here used to indicate a small enclosure.

l. 24: County Clare: In western Ireland, on the Atlantic, between Galway Bay and the River Shannon; S of Co. Galway.

ll. 27-28: "Dublin . . . Post Office": A center of fighting during the 1916 Easter Rising against British sovereignty.

l. 33: coracle: A small boat of ancient lineage, originally made of hide stretched over a wicker frame; to-day, hoop-ribbed, the covering either hide or tarpaulin.

P. 278, l. 1: Muckanish: Island off the Connemara coast.

l. 2: Finvara: Finavarra: Village and point of land east of Ballyvaghan.

P. 279, l. 8: Aughanish: *V.* notes to *The Unicorn*. . . .—Bailevelehan: Really Ballyvaghan, in northern part of Co. Clare.

l. 9: Aughtmana: ? Possibly a village on Aughinish Island.

P. 280, l. 19: Kerry: County in southwestern Ireland, its capital Tralee.—Connacht: Anciently *Connachta*, Medb's kingdom in W of Ireland.

l. 22: Donough O'Brien: ? Sixteenth-century 2d Earl of Thomond.

l. 24: Thomond: Now eastern part of Co. Clare.

P. 282, Young Girl's first speech: Perhaps the worst bit of syntax in all Yeats!

l. 24: Helen: Helen of Troy.

l. 34: Diarmuid and Dervorgilla: *V.* Mac-Manus, 321 ff.; cp. Standish James O'Grady's *The Departure of Dermot*, L. Gregory's *Dervorgilla*.

P. 283, l. 13: Connemara: A wild mountainous region in western Co. Galway; cp. L. Gregory, *OIT*, 11.

P. 284, song, st. 2: "wandering": A favorite adjective of Yeats's youth, probably out of Shelley.

N.B. It seems that the historical Dervorgilla (wife of Tigernan O'Rourke) was past forty when she eloped with Diarmuid Mac Murrough, king of Leinster (and then past sixty)!

Yeats told Lady Gregory this play was "too strong, politically" (Wade, 629). The title recalls the "Dreaming Back," Bk. III of *A Vision, q.v. V.* also Yeats's "Note" in 56 or 61, and cp. his early story "Hanrahan's Vision."—Cp. Peacock, 124-25.—McGreevy (32) seems alone in asserting this was [as late as 1929] Yeats's favorite among his plays.

CALVARY

1: Incorrectly dated: earliest publication, 1921.

2a: 56, 61, 73, 87.—Best available text (1957), 87E. Except for one or two minor corrections, play assumed final form in 61. (The original version makes the Second Roman Soldier's last speech a simple "Begin the dance" and has some purely technical errors; the soldier's speech is lengthened in 61; the final version revises four other lines.)

b: No record.

3: No record.

4: On the (?) supernatural interruption of Yeats's reading of this play at Gogarty's home, *v.* Wade, 729-30.— Cp. *At the Hawk's Well, supra.*

5: *Gloss*:

P. 289, bottom: Lazarus: Cp. John 11:11-44.

P. 291, l. 2: Cp. Luke 10:38-42; Matthew 27:56; John 19:25; etc.—Song: For concluding l., cp. Dionysian association, Yeats's preface to *A Full Moon in March;* also conclusion of Sc. V, *The Herne's Egg.*

P. 292, Judas' second speech: For a New Testament reference, violated by Yeats's conception, *v., e.g.,* Matthew 27:3-5.—Third Roman Soldier's second speech: Cp. Matthew 27:35.

P. 293, Third Music.: "one-eyed day": Note sun

image. Cp. Shakespeare's "eye of heaven" (Sonnet XVIII).

Second l. from bottom: Cp. Villon's "But where are the snows of yesteryear?" (*Ballade of Dead Ladies,* Rossetti trans.)

For the bird symbolism, *v.* Yeats's note on the play in 61 (A, 471 ff.).—On the Lazarus episode, cp. Wilde's story recorded on p. 171 of the *Auto.*—Cp. Henn, 267-70. One may also cp. pp. 186-87 of the 1925 version of *A Vision.*

THE CAT AND THE MOON

1: Incorrectly dated: earliest publication, 1924.
2a: *The Criterion* and *The Dial,* July 1924; 65 (with interesting preface and notes), 72 (with rpt. of Yeats's intro.), 73, 87.—The 87 texts are best. The play assumes final form in 72, with minor changes in punctuation, revision of the Martyn-Moore portion, and addition of the final twelve bits of dialogue as the most essential alterations.—On the lyric, *v.* "The Cat and the Moon" (85, 86, or 88) and *Proleg. I.*
b: No record.
3: 21 Sept. 1931; Abbey Theatre, Dublin; by Abbey Co.
—according to Robinson, *IAT,* which gives the cast

on p. 146. McNamara is in agreement, but Yeats, in 72, dates the earliest production 9 May 1926; however, Yeats's dating is sometimes far from reliable.

4: This is dated 1917 in 65, whose "Notes" (p. 35) say Yeats originally wrote it "with the intention of including it in 'Four Plays for Dancers,' but did not do so as it was in a different mood." We also find, "Minnaloushe and the Moon were perhaps—it all grows faint to me—an exposition of man's relation to what I have called the Antithetical Tincture, and when the Saint mounts upon the back of the Lame Beggar he personifies a certain great spiritual event which may take place when Primary Tincture . . . supersedes Antithetical. . . ." The implied reference is to *A Vision*: but cp. also later comment.—The introduction to the 72 printing is convenient for the symbolism.

5: *Gloss*:

P. 296, open. dia., l. 3: St. Colman's well was within "a couple of miles" of Thoor Ballylee, Yeats's tower in Co. Galway ("Notes," 65; p. 36). Yeats (*Idem*) relates the play vaguely to "some story . . . half forgotten, of a lame man and a blind man's arrival at it." (St. Colman mac Lenin was the patron saint of the now-ruined Cathedral Church of Kilmacduagh, near Coole.)

P. 298, fifth l. from bottom: Laban: A village between Kiltartan and Ardrahan, Co. Galway.—Presumably the "big house" is to suggest Martyn's Tulira Castle.

second l. from bottom: Mayo: County of George Moore's birth, and of Moore Hall; N of Co. Galway.

P. 300, Blind Beggar's first speech: "I see it all

now . . .": Cp. Martin Doul, in Synge's *Well of the Saints*, after his (temporary) cure from blindness.

Cp. *Auto.*, 243-44; §IV, "Intro.," 72: identification of Edward Martyn as "the holy man in the big house at Laban" and of George Moore as the "old lecher."—Cp. Peacock, 121-22.

SOPHOCLES' KING OEDIPUS

1: Correctly dated for earliest publication.
2a: 67, 73, 87.—87 is the best set of texts, with A as good as E except (1957) for an "Oh" improperly replacing the "Ah" at the beginning of the Messenger's eighth speech on p. 319. The 67 text has, as compared with that of 87, less naturalness in certain bits of dialogue, more faulty punctuation, and the misspelling of some Greek names; it also lists some nonspeaking parts and is accompanied by "The Music for the Chorus."
b: No record.
3: 7 Dec. 1926; Abbey Theatre, Dublin; by Abbey Co.— For cast, *v.* Robinson, *IAT*, 140. Yeats called this production a "great success" (Wade, 720).
4: This play was, with its sequel, a matter of concern

for many years.—On 1911-12 efforts to make a version, *v.* Hone, 273-74; for elaboration, and the method of producing the versions (Yeats very honestly does not call them "translations") finally achieved, *v.* the very important footnote in Wade, 537, and cp. pp. 538-39, 546, 710, 714, and—for a reported bit of supernaturalism—729. On Antheil's musical setting, *v., Idem,* 760; on Yeats's preproduction comment, cp. Hone, 413-14.

5: *Gloss*:

Sophocles: A major Greek dramatist; b. 495, d. 406 B.C.

P. 304, l. 1: Cadmus: Phoenician prince, brother of Europa; reputed inventor of letters, builder of the Theban citadel, and ruler of Thebes by assignment of the goddess Athena.

l. 10: Zeus: Supreme Olympian god.

l. 11: "market-places": One in each division of the city, which was cut by the River Strophia.

l. 18: "harsh singer, the riddling Sphinx": Presumably called a "singer" because of chanting the riddle, which ran (*Smaller Class. Dict., cit.,* 365): "A being with four feet has two feet and three feet, and only one voice; but its feet vary, and when it has most it is weakest." With this riddle the winged creature (half woman, half lioness), sitting outside Thebes, used to accost passers-by, slaying all who could not solve it. When Oedipus defined the "being" as man (in babyhood, upright prime, and bestaffed old age), the sphinx committed suicide.

P. 305, l. 13: "Pythian House of Phoebus": "Phoebus" ("bright") was an epithet of the god

Apollo—god of (among other things) prophecy, and slayer of the serpent Python. Delphi was anciently called Pytho.

last l.: Delphi: Town in Phocis, famous for its oracle of Apollo.

P. 306, *Chorus* (composed of noble Theban elders): St. 1: "Delian" God: Apollo, son of Zeus and Leto, was born at Delos, where his great temple stood.
St. 2: "God of Death": Ares is here indicated.—"western shore": As often also in Celtic tradition, the sphere of the Otherworld.

P. 307, *Chorus,* St. 4: Artemis: Goddess; twin of Apollo.—Maenads: μαίνομαι: "the mad": The Bacchantes, frenzied in worship of Dionysus (Bacchus).—"Lysian": A surname of Apollo.

l. 21: "Pythian God": Apollo.

P. 310, Tiresias' second speech: "Loxias": Another surname of Apollo.

P. 311, *Chorus*: Parnassus: A mountain range, its highest peak N of Delphi.—"navel of the world": Delphi, regarded by the Greeks as the center of the earth. In its temple of Apollo was a small chasm, intermittently emissive of intoxicating vapors. After inhaling and exhaling these vapors, the priestess (Pythia) would deliver oracles supposedly from Apollo.

P. 314, l. 10: Helios: God of the sun.

P. 315, Jocasta's third speech: "Daulia": Daulis, another town in Phocis.

P. 317, *Chorus:* St. 3: "Delphian Sibyl": The Pythia. —"world's navel-stone": Cp. *supra.*

P. 320, Messenger's sixth speech: Cithaeron: Mountain range separating Attica and Megaris from

Boeotia; tenth speech: "the spancel": This means the feet had been pierced and bound together; their resultant swollen condition suggested the name "Oedipus."

P. 321, *Chorus:* Helicon: Boeotian mountain range, sacred to Apollo.—"Lord Pan": God of herds, flocks, pastures, etc.—"mountain Lord": Dionysus.—*N.B.* The last 4 ll. represent fanciful speculation on the possibility of a supernatural origin for Oedipus.

P. 324, *Chorus:* Last st.: "woman-breasted Fate": The Greek (as distinguished from the Egyptian) sphinx.

Sec. Messenger's first speech: Ister: Ancient name of lower Danube River.—Phasis: A river of Colchis, associated with a god so named.

P. 325, ll. 4-7: Cp. Tiresias' prophecy, p. 309.

Cp. anonymous *Herald Tribune* art.; Henn, 266-67.

SOPHOCLES'
OEDIPUS AT COLONUS

1: Correctly dated for earliest publication.
2a: 73, 87.—The 87E text is (1957) best.
 b: No record.

3: 12 Sept. 1927; Abbey Theatre, Dublin; by Abbey Co. —For cast, *v.* Robinson, *IAT*, 141.—On the "phantom dog," *v.* Wade, 729; on Antheil's music, *Idem,* 760.

4: Wade (720 fn. 4) says Yeats was at work on this when *Oedipus the King* was produced; one should cp. also, *Idem,* 721.

5. *Gloss:*

(*N.B.* Colonus, a mile or so NW of Athens, was Sophocles' birthplace.)

P. 330, l. 8: "distant towers": Presumably the Athenian Acropolis.

P. 331, Stranger's third speech: "pleasanter names": E.g., the euphemistic "Eumenides" ("well-intentioned").—Stranger's seventh speech: Poseidon: God of the sea and of horses (the first of which he reputedly created); Prometheus: Really a cousin to Zeus: the name means "forethought"; "the Brazen Threshold" (cp. last speech, p. 359): Supposedly fronted the opening into Hades; "Lord of the Manor": Hardly a classical phrase! —Stranger's tenth speech: Theseus: Slayer of the Minotaur.

P. 332, Oedipus' second speech: "When he proclaimed . . .": i.e., in Oedipus' youth, at Delphi.

P. 334, l. 6: "Labdacidae": Because descended from Labdacus, Oedipus' grandfather.

P. 339, l. 2: "three streams of water": The Sophoclean original has the third bowl containing a mixture of honey and water.

Chorus' fourth speech: "Good People": Eumenides, so-called out of fear; cp. Irish phrase for *faeries.*

P. 341, Oedipus' twelfth speech: Hellas: Greece.

P. 343, *Chorus:* Cp. "Colonus' Praise," *Proleg. I.*

    St. 1: "wine-dark": Homeric epithet.— "wood's": That of the Eumenides.—"Immortal ladies": The nymphs.—"Semele's lad": Dionysus, god of wine, was the son of Zeus and Semele, daughter of Cadmus.

    St. 2: "Miracle-bred": The olive was supposedly Athena's creation.—". . . nor war": Even the Spartans respected the olive.—Athene (Athena): Guardian deity of Athens; daughter of Zeus and Metis.

    St. 3: "Who comes": The Persian invader. —"Great Mother . . .": Demeter, mourning for Persephone, abducted by Hades while gathering the narcissus.—Cephisus: A stream flowing from Mt. Pentelicus past Athens.

    St. 4: "Poseidon gave it bit and oar": As creator of the horse and god of the sea.

P. 350, *Chorus:* "Pythian strand": Shore of Eleusis. —Oea: Apparently never identified.—"son of Rhea": Poseidon.—Apollo and Artemis: Twin deities.

P. 353, *Chorus:* Cp. "A Man Young and Old," XI, *Proleg. I.*

P. 354, mid-portion of Polyneices' speech: "Seven leaders . . .": These were all killed in battle, and the expedition failed; cp. Aeschylus' *Seven against Thebes.*

P. 356, ll. 5-6: V. Sophocles' *Antigone.*

P. 358, sixth l. from bottom: "the dragon's teeth": Descendants of the five survivors of the armed men who sprang up and fought when, directed by Athena, Cadmus sowed the teeth of the slain dragon-guardian of a well at the founding of Thebes.

P. 359, l. 5: "Goddess of the Dead": Persephone.

Chorus: St. 1: Hades: Uncle and husband of Persephone, and brother of Zeus; euphemistically called "Pluto" ("wealth-giver").—Furies: The Erinyes (Avengers).—"Stygian": The Styx was the main river of Hades, the Greek Underworld.

St. 2: "hundred-headed dog": Cerberus, guardian of the entrance to Hades; of the spawn of Echidna and the monster Typhon.—"the daughter of Earth and Tartarus": Echidna—half woman, half serpent; child of Tartarus by his mother, Gē.

P. 359, fifth l. from bottom: "stone from Thoricus": Apparently never identified.

P. 360, l. 1: "dress the dead": i.e., in white.

THE RESURRECTION

1: Incorrectly dated for earliest publication. Magazine publication took place in 1927, after which reworking preceded book publication in 1932. (Perhaps the fact that 68 was "finished" in 1931 accounts for Yeats's dating.)

2a: *The Adelphi,* June 1927; 68: new version, 72, 73, 87.—
Either of the 87 texts is satisfactory. [On the opening
and closing songs, *v.* "Two Songs from a Play" (85,
86, or 88) and *Proleg. I.*]—The original version is
much more inchoate—is almost suggestive of the half-
confused; the final is a thoroughly reworked piece:
more compact, more logical in progression, though
perhaps slightly less clearly explanatory of the
Dionysian rites. Yeats's introduction is reprinted in
72, the version which, collations suggest, was probably revised later than that of 73. Incidentally, "The
Greek" is "The Egyptian" in *The Adelphi* list of per-
sons, though referred to by "The Syrian" as "almost a
Greek."

b: No record.

3: 30 July 1934; Abbey Theatre, Dublin; by Abbey Co.:
shared bill with *King of the Great Clock Tower.*—
For cast, *v.* Robinson, *IAT,* 159.

4: This was drafted in 1925, but unsympathetically re-
ceived on a reading to friends at 82 Merrion Square,
Dublin (Hone, 446); on ideas supposedly nourishing
it, one may consult Yeats's introduction (especially
Section 3) in 72. Yeats was apparently absorbed with
prose drafts for the lyrics in Jan. of 1929 (cp. Hone,
430); he was "putting the last touches" to his reworking of the play on 27 Dec. 1930 (cp. Wade, 780), and
he writes of rehearsals, 24 July 1934 (*Idem,* 826).—
This is the most thoroughly reworked of Yeats's plays
postdating *The Unicorn . . . ,* the curious *Clock Tower*
pieces aside.

5: *Gloss:*

P. 365, Greek's last speech: "thirteen": Christ and

the twelve disciples.—Hebrew's last speech: Cp. Matthew 26:26-28.

P. 366, first six ll.: Cp. Matthew 26:69-75.

P. 367, Hebrew's first speech: Cp. Isaiah 7:14 and 11:1.

P. 368, song: "Astrea": ? Astræa: goddess of justice: sometimes regarded as the daughter of the Titan Astræus by Eos; in her heavenly transformation, Virgo.—This goddess seems indicated by the last stanza, though I have found no tradition making her the mother of Dionysus.

P. 370, Syrian's second and third speeches: Cp. Matthew 28:1-10; Mark 16:1-13.—Syrian's last speech: Cp. Matthew 27:66.

P. 371, first six ll.: Cp. Matthew 28.—Syrian's fifth speech: Hone (447) glosses *The Hour-Glass:* ". . . belief comes from shock."

P. 372, Syrian's last speech: Cp. John 21:19-28.

P. 373: Heraclitus: Ephesian philosopher, early sixth century B.C.; held fire to be the primary element, with everything in flux (πάντα ῥεῖ).

McGreevy, apparently writing in 1929, counted this Yeats's greatest play and claimed (35) that it "makes the greatest miracle of Christianity credible."

THE WORDS UPON THE WINDOW-PANE

1: Correctly dated for earliest publication.

2a: 71, 72, 73, 78, 87.—Either of the 87 texts is satisfactory.—Here, again, the text of 72 seems to have been prepared later than that of 73, publication dates notwithstanding.

   N.B. "The Words upon the Window Pane: A Commentary" first appeared in the *Dublin Magazine*, Oct.-Dec. 1931 and Jan.-Mar. 1932 nos.—V. "Fragments," I (85, 86, or 88), and *Proleg. I.*

 b: No record.

3: 17 Nov. 1930; Abbey Theatre, Dublin; by Abbey Co. —For cast, *v.* Robinson, *IAT*, 145.

4: *V.* Yeats's lengthy "Introduction" (dated 1931) in 72. —In a footnote to p. 891 of the *Letters*, Wade says that the fact that in 1910 Yeats, living in "Fairfield," one of Gogarty's houses, found an inscription cut with a diamond on a bedroom window-pane "gave rise" eventually to this play. It was finished (at Coole) before 23 Oct. 1930 (Wade, 777) and in rehearsal by 29 Oct. (*Idem,* 778).

5: *Gloss*:

   P. 376, l. 2: Ballymoney: The best-known Ballymoney is probably the linen, dairy, and pork products center in northwestern Co. Antrim; but the name also labels "a small country parish ten miles West of Bandon, in the County of Cork," where Lennox Robinson (14) says his father was once rector.

P. 377, l. 3: *Human Personality:* A 2-vol. work by F. W. H. Meyers pub. in 1903.—Conan Doyle: Sir Arthur (1859–1930), creator of Sherlock Holmes; the "wild book": ? *A New Revelation* (1918)—? *History of Spiritualism* (2 vols., 1926).

l. 7: David Home: Obviously an error for *Daniel D. Home* (1833–86), Scotch spiritualist and medium.

Dr. Trench's fourth speech: Harold's Cross: Dog-racing track in suburb of that name southwest of Dublin.

last paragraph: Grattan: Henry: eighteenth-century Irish Parliamentarian.—Curran: John Philpot (1780–1817): Irish orator, judge, Parliamentarian, and defender of Napper Tandy.—Stella: Esther Johnson. For a concise, sane comment, *v.* Sampson, 466-68.

P. 378, Corbet's first speech: Vanessa: Hester Vanhomrigh.

P. 379, l. 6: Bolingbroke: Henry St. John, 1st Viscount (1678–1751): English statesman.—Harley: Robert, Earl of Oxford; friend (before rival) of Bolingbroke.—Ormonde: James Butler, 2d Duke (1665–1745): Military commander in William III's army, serving at the Boyne; twice lord lieutenant of Ireland.

Corbet's speech: Brutus: Marcus Junius (85–42 B.C.): Roman politician; one of Julius

Caesar's assassins.—Cato: Marcus Porcius (95–46 B.C.), "the Younger": Roman philosopher-patriot.—Rousseau: Jean Jacques (1712–88): French author-philosopher.—*saeva indignatio:* "savage indignation" (from Swift's epitaph).

Johnson's speech: Moody: Dwight L.: A nineteenth-century American evangelist, as was also Sankey.

P. 380, Dr. Trench's first speech: Cp. Bk. III, *A Vision;* "Crazy Jane on God" (85, 86, or 88; and *Proleg. I*); *Purgatory;* Wellesley, 191.

Dr. Trench's second speech: *requiescat in pace:* "he rests in peace."

P. 383, l. 15: Plutarch: Greek biographer (?46–?120).

P. 384, l. 4: Dr. Arbuthnot: John (1667–1735).

P. 385, next-to-last l.: Chrysostom: St. John, Greek church father (?347–407).

P. 387, 1st stage directions: Yeats credits this touch to his wife, who is in the *1930 Diary* said to have urged the writing of this play.

P. 388, last sent.: "Perish the day on which I was born!"—*Job*, 3:3: "Let the day perish wherein I was born. . . ."

L. A. G. Strong counted this Yeats's best play. Cp. Robinson, 70-72; Jeffares, 19.

A FULL MOON IN MARCH

1: Correctly dated.
2a: *Poetry* (Chicago), Mar. 1935; 76, 80, 87.—The book versions are all satisfactory, though the first song on p. 395 of 87A should be printed in two four-line stanzas. (87E is also in error on this score.) In the *Poetry* version there are three undescribed attendants, though the third has no dialogue; the opening passages are in prose; and the stage directions vary somewhat. The reworking in 76 reflects clear improvement, not only in punctuation, but also in a tightening and condensation of dialogue here and there; it became the final text except for minor changes in placement of initial stage directions and two or three changes in punctuation.
b: No record.
3: No record.
4: Yeats refers to this, a work begun about six years earlier than its date of completion (Wade, 830), as "blood symbolism"; and admits on 28 Nov. 1935, "I don't like it" (*Idem*, 843—and cp. 844). In the "Preface" to 76 he says he reworked it from *The King of the Great Clock Tower* for the sake of "greater intensity."—V. Wilson, Chs. I and II.

5: *Gloss*:
> P. 390, ll. 5-6 of song: Pythagoras: sixth century B.C.
> Greek philosopher.
> P. 392, l. 17: Cp. l. 8, p. 409.

Cp. Henn, 270-72; *The Resurrection* (second speech of "The Greek," 87A, 368); §IX, Bk. II, *A Vision*. One may also consult the closing passages of Bentley's uneven and in some respects highly debatable essay.

THE KING OF THE GREAT CLOCK TOWER

1: Correctly dated for earliest publication of this version, though the prose version came in 1934.—Since Yeats prints in 73 the acting version of *The Shadowy Waters* and recommends ("Preface," 76) for production purposes the prose version of *KGCT*, it seems curious that the verse version of the second play is the one chosen for inclusion in 87. However, one notes that in 87 *The Countess Cathleen* is also (and happily) not given in the acting version.

2a: *Prose Version: Life and Letters,* Oct. 1934; 74 (cp. intro. and notes), 75.

Verse Version: 76, 80, 87.—The verse versions agree except in that the "Stroller" of 87 is a "Stranger" in 76 and 80.

b: No record.
3: ?—*N.B.* The prose version was produced 30 July 1934 (Yeats is in error in 74) at the Abbey, together with *The Resurrection;* Robinson gives the cast, *IAT,* 159.—Cp. Wade, 826-27—and also 830, where Yeats calls the play "theatrically coherent, spiritually incoherent."
4: Begun in Nov. 1933 (cp. Wade, 754, 817), this was apparently finished by 27 Jan. 1934 (*Idem,* 819; cp. 845).—Yeats ("Preface," 76) says "a friend [obviously Ezra Pound] . . . denounced it in violent language" after a reading. On the singing of the severed head, *v.* the "Commentary," 74: Yeats relates it to a story in the initial edition of *The Secret Rose* (1897). On the "Alternative Song," for which Arthur Duff provided a tune, *v.* 85, 86, or 88, and *Proleg. I.*—V. Wilson, Chs. I and II.
5: *Gloss:*
　　P. 398, l. 1: Tir-nan-oge: *Tír-na-nÓg,* Celtic "Land of the Young": the happy Otherworld.
　　　　l. 3: "speech of birds": Cp. the song of the dead in "Cuchulain Comforted" (85, 86, or 88).
　　　　l. 8: Cp. "His Bargain" (85, 86, or 88) and *Proleg. I.*
　　　　ll. 10-16: Cp. "The Wanderings of Oisin," I (85, 86, or 88), and *Proleg. I.*
　　P. 401, l. 12: In prose version, addressed to Queen.
　　　　ll. 24-25: Cp. prose version: "Ah, that is better. But sing out loud that all here may know that you rejoice in his death."
　　P. 403, l. 9: V. notes to *The King's Threshold.*
V. again Henn, 270-72.

THE HERNE'S EGG

1: Correctly dated.

2a: 79, 80, 87.—The best text (1957) is 87E.

b: V. Wade *Biblio.*, 366.

3: No record.

4: This play was being pondered when Yeats wrote to Dorothy Wellesley on 28 Nov. 1935 (Wade, 843), and was begun shortly afterward at Palma, Majorca (*Idem,* 755). The scenario was finished 20 Dec., and the verse was begun the next day (*Idem,* 845). The Abbey at first planned production (*Idem,* 868), but quickly changed its mind (? early Dec. 1936), to Yeats's apparent relief, since he had feared rioting (*Idem,* 871): nevertheless, in sending Ethel Mannin a copy, 17 Feb. 1938, he wrote: "It disturbed the Abbey board until I withdrew it. An admiring member had decided that the seven ravishers of the heroine are the seven sacraments." (This after calling it "very Rabelasian" but cautioning, "do not ask me what it means": *Idem,* 904-5.)—Hone (495) calls it "too ribald to be produced", but Yeats makes clear his own high opinion of it in his letters to Dorothy Wellesley.—V. Wilson, Chs. I and III.

5: *Gloss*:

Tara (in Meath) was the seat of the High Kings of Ireland.

P. 409, l. 8: *V.* notes to *A Full Moon.* . . .

P. 417, l. 14: Flippant reference to the "Great Wheel" of *A Vision?*

P. 422, l. 25: ? Cp. Yeats's preface to 76.

P. 423, Sc. VI: In the original version, the moon is only about to rise—and is rising just before the seventeenth bit of dialogue before the end is spoken.

Cp. Strong (*Scattering Branches,* ed. Gwynn; 213); O'Connor; Pearce; London *Times Lit. Supp.,* 22 Jan. 1938. —Henn, 272, should be considered, though I fear his reading may here be doubtful and his interpretation somewhat strained.

The *herne* is, of course, a type of heron.

PURGATORY

1: Correctly dated.

2a: 81, 82, 83, 87.—The best texts are those of 87.

  b: No record.

3: 10 Aug. 1938; Abbey Theatre, Dublin; by Abbey Co., with settings by poet's daughter.—For cast, *v.* Robinson, *IAT,* 166.—Cp. Wade, 913-14-15; Hone, 506.

4: This is dated Apr. 1938 in 82; the poet was brooding on it in mid-March of that year (Wade, 907: a foot-

note says Yeats began it at Chantrey House, the home
of Edith Shackleton Heald and her sister, Steyning,
Sussex; and May seems implied as the date on p. 756
of the *Letters*).—On a Yeats ghost story of possible
relationship, *v*. Hone, 302-3.

The ideational roots of the play are clearly in *The
Words upon the Window-Pane*, "Anima Mundi," and
A Vision (cp. §XXXIX, *1930 Diary*). Cp. "Three
Songs to the One Burden," I:

> The common breeds the common,
> A lout begets a lout—

V. Wilson, Chs. I and IV.
5: *Gloss*:
P. 433, ll. 18-21: Cp. §XXXIX, *1930 Diary*.
P. 435, l. 1: Cp. "Crazy Jane on God" (85, 86, or
88) and *Proleg. I*.

Cp. Ellmann, 276; Pearce; and MacNeice, who not surprisingly counts this and *The Death of Cuchulain* "flat
failures" (*op. cit.*, 862).

THE DEATH OF CUCHULAIN

1: Correctly dated.
2a: 81, 83, 87.—87E is (1957) the best text, but this has a couple of faults in punctuation in which it agrees with 87A, where p. 440 should have a colon in place of the semicolon of l. 6 and l. 24 of p. 444 should end with a question mark. (Cp. 83.)
 b: No record.
 3: According to Mrs. Bjersby, "First performed at the Abbey Theatre in 1949, by Austin Clarke's Lyric Theatre." Details not available.
 4: According to Hone (509), Yeats made a prose draft of this "at Chantry House" [sic] (v. Purgatory, supra) before leaving for the Riviera in the fall of 1938; certainly he was working on it before 20 Oct. 1938 (Wade, 917-18) and apparently finished it at Cap Martin before Christmas (cp., Idem, 921). He wrote of it (Idem, 922) as "strange and the most moving I have written for some years."—V. Wilson, Chs. I and V.
 5: Gloss:
 On Emer, Eithne, Maeve, Aoife, Conall Cearnach, and Conchubar, v. notes on At the Hawk's Well,

The Green Helmet, On Baile's Strand, and *The Only Jealousy of Emer.*

P. 439, l. 12: Degas: Hilaire Germaine Edgar (1834–1917): French painter.

l. 15: Rameses the Great: Ancient Egyptian king.

l. 21: Emain Macha: Capital of Uladh, SW of Armagh; said to have been destroyed in A.D. 332. For two legendary explanations of its founding, *v.* Keating, II, 153-57.

P. 440, Cuchulain's last speech: Cp. "Cuchulain's Fight with the Sea" (85, 86, or 88) and *The Only Jealousy of Emer.*

P. 442, l. 3: Tradition says Cuchulain overthrew Aoife partly by trickery.

l. 19: "The grey of Macha": A kelpie (lakehorse), and one of Cuchulain's two chariot horses.

P. 443, ll. 17 ff.: Presumably Yeatsian invention.

l. 27: One fancies that Yeats would have revised this line had he lived.

P. 444, l. 28: Cp. "Cuchulain Comforted" (85, 86, or 88).

P. 445, l. 10: "Usna's boys": Naoise, Ainnle, and Ardan; *v.* Deirdre story.

P. 446, l. 1: "in the Post Office": During the Easter Rising, 1916; Dublin.

l. 2: Pearse: Padraic: *V.* "Easter 1916," *Proleg. I.*

l. 3: Connolly: James: With Pearse, one of the leaders executed by the British after the 1916 Rising.

Cp. Ure, 23; Pearce; Henn, 277-80.—With Yeats's fable,

largely a contrivance of his own, cp. Nutt's summary, quoted in Saul, 83-86.

This play completes Yeats's "dramatic celebration of the life of Cuchulain" proposed in *Certain Noble Plays of Japan*.

APPENDIX *I: NOTES ON UNCOLLECTED OR UNPUBLISHED DRAMA*

1a. *Vivien and Time.* Pref. poem dated in MS 8 Jan. 1884 (Ellmann, Ch. III).—V. "Time and the Witch Vivien," 2, 2a: rptd. in 88.

b. *Love and Death.* Unpub. MS. Apr. 1884 (Ellmann, *ibid.*).

2. *The Island of Statues. An Arcadian Faery Tale. In Two Acts.* Dublin Univ. Rev., Apr.-July 1885.— Act II, Sc. iii, as "Island of Statues," 2, 2a.—Cp. Wade, 117-18.—Rpt. in 88.

   N.B. V. McHugh, 90, *re* 1a and 2, *supra*.

3. *The Seeker. A Dramatic Poem. In Two Scenes.* Dublin Univ. Rev., Sept. 1885; as "The Seeker," 2, 2a.— Rpt. in 88.

   N.B. "An Epilogue. To The Island of Statues and The Seeker." *Dublin Univ. Rev.*, Oct. 1885.—V. "The Song of the Happy Shepherd" (85, 86, or 88) and *Proleg. I.*

4. *Mosada. A Dramatic Poem.* Dublin Univ. Rev., June 1886 (but written before *The Island of Statues*); 1: as offprint of preceding (Dublin: Sealy, Bryers, and Walker), Yeats's father and E. Dowden having found subscribers (Hone, 52): cp. Wade *Biblio.*

(It. 1); 2, 2a, 83: as ltd. edn. based on 2, with corrections from Yeats's copy.—MS dated 7 June 1886:
v. Wade *Biblio.,* It. 206.—V. rpt. in 88.

5. *Diarmuid and Grania* (with George Moore). Pub. by
William Becker, *Dublin Magazine,* Apr.-June no.,
1951.—On genesis and collaboration, *v.* Wade, 326,
347-48, 368 (on a new second act: early in 1902).
Yeats hoped to rework this play in his own way:
v. 13 Nov. 1904 letter to Frank Fay (Wade, 443).—
Prod. 21 Oct. 1901 by Frank Benson's Co. for the
"Irish Literary Theatre," Gaiety Theatre, Dublin.
For cast and history of production, *v.* Robinson,
IAT, 20-24.—Cp. D. Gwynn, 136; Lady Gregory,
OIT, 28-29; Jeffares, 9-10; Moore, *H&F,* I, 281-84,
356-78, and II, 105-9, 111-13.

6. Unpub. MS: *V.* Adams.

APPENDIX *II: NOTE ON FIRST AMERICAN PRINTING OF DEFINITIVE* COLLECTED PLAYS

Students using the first printing of 87A (the only one available at time of present writing) should be aware of the following errors, whether or not these constitute a complete list, for which eventual correction is anticipated:

The Countess Cathleen:

> P. 5, First word, l. 3, of Cathleen's 4th speech: "But" should be "By."
>
> P. 19, l. 5 of First Merchant's 3d speech: "Come" should be "Came."
>
> P. 29, l. 7 of Aleel's 2d speech: "in" should be "is."
>
> P. 30: The first set of stage directions should end with a period or a colon (cp. 1912 version and *Plays and Controversies*), not a semicolon. (Error also in 87E.)

The Land of Heart's Desire: V. §4 of the notes on this play, *supra.*

Cathleen Ni Houlihan:

> P. 56: The mid-page song should have a stanzaic break after the 4th line.

The Pot of Broth:

> P. 64, l. 2: "furzy" should be "furze."

The King's Threshold:

P. 75, l. 5 of 2d stage directions: The inverted comma is missing before *Ireland*.

P. 77, l. 21: "hand" should be "hands."

P. 91, l. 2 of Seanchan's 1st speech: "Who had" should be "Who have."

P. 92: Third line from bottom should end with period, not comma.

The Shadowy Waters:

P. 108: The comma ending the 3d line of Forgael's 3d speech should be a semicolon.

P. 125, l. 2 of Deirdre's 1st speech: "heighty" should be "haughty."

P. 129, l. 2 of Deirdre's 1st speech: The comma should be a period.

At the Hawk's Well:

P. 138, l. 14: "top" should be "tap."

Passim: The spelling "Sualtam" (cp. earlier texts of the play and 87E) is more conventional than "Sualtim."

The Green Helmet:

P. 156, l. 2: "right of the place" should be "right of place."

On Baile's Strand:

P. 166, l. 1 of Blind Man's 1st speech: "something" should be "somebody."

P. 169, l. 5 of Conchubar's 3d speech: "have" should be "had."

l. 1 of Conchubar's 4th speech: "that" should be "but."

P. 171, 9th l. from bottom: "will" should be deleted.

P. 173, last word: "kings" should not be capitalized.

The Hour-Glass:

V. first item in gloss to *Hour-Glass, supra.*

P. 206, l. 4 of Fourth Pupil's last speech: "know" should be "knew."

P. 207, 4th line from bottom: Should read, "My pupils said that they would find a man."

P. 208, last line: "children" should not be capitalized.

P. 210, l. 2 of 6th speech from bottom: "have seen" should be "had seen."

P. 210, l. 2 of succeeding speech (by Fool): "give" should be "gives."

The Unicorn from the Stars:

P. 216, l. 1: "gold" should be "golden."

P. 218, l. 1 of Thomas' last speech: "a" should be inserted before "trance".

P. 219, l. 2 of Thomas' 2d speech: "to" should be inserted after "on."

P. 221, l. 12: The periods should be commas.

P. 222, l. 2 of Andrew's 1st speech: Yeats apparently spelled "traveling" with two *ll*'s.

P. 224: Andrew's 3d speech: The speaker's name should be italicized and "Whisht" should be followed by an exclamation point, not a question mark.

8th l. from bottom: Final bracket and period should be transposed.

P. 229, 1st stage directions: "Nanny grabs it" should be "Nanny grabs at it."

P. 231, Martin's 3d speech: "best" should be inserted after "is." (Incidentally, *Plays in Prose and Verse* has a very logical "me" after "tell," though this is missing from 73A and 87E, whether through oversight or by intention.)

P. 233, Johnny's 1st speech: "make" should be "made."

P. 235: Johnny's 2d speech should end with an exclamation point.

P. 244, Thomas' 2d speech: "Hurray" should be "Hurry."

P. 245, last line: The comma after "breast" should be a period.

P. 246, l. 3 of Johnny's 2d speech: "hanging" should be "hanged."

The Player Queen:

P. 250, Second Man's last speech: "for" should be "by."

P. 253, Septimus' 1st speech: "a" should be inserted before "milk-white horn."

P. 256, Second Old Man's 1st speech: Though omission may not indicate an error, one wonders whether "soon" should not be inserted before "begin," as in three earlier editions, though it is missing from 73A and 87E.

P. 268, 2d line from bottom: "darlings" should be "darling."

The Dreaming of the Bones:

P. 282, l. 5 of Young Girl's 2d speech: "a" should be inserted before "husband's."

P. 283, l. 14 of dialogue: "The Galway" should be "And Galway."

Calvary:

P. 290, l. 3 of Lazarus' 3d speech: "done" should be "gone."

Sophocles' King Oedipus:

P. 319, l. 9 from bottom: "Oh, my son . . ." should be "Ah, my son. . . ."

Sophocles' Oedipus at Colonus:

P. 332, Oedipus' 4th speech: "that" should be "but."

P. 344, l. 11 from bottom: "then it was" should be "then, then it was."

P. 345, Oedipus' 4th speech should open: "Begone, I tell you to be gone . . ."

P. 348, 1. 7: "dealt" should be "dealt out"; 1. 16: "not" should be "nor"; 1. 20: "know how" should be "know better how."

P. 353, st. 3, 1. 1, of Chorus: "streets" should be "street." 3d line from bottom: The semicolon after "father" should be a colon.

P. 354, 1. 1: The colon should be a semicolon.

P. 356: The last comma of 1. 2 should be a semicolon.— Antigone's 6th speech: "So" should be followed by a comma.

P. 360, 1. 4: "down upon" should be "down at."

P. 361, 6th line from end: "He had" should be "He laid."

The Resurrection and *The Words upon the Window-Pane:* Many sets of brackets in the stage directions are left incomplete, as sometimes elsewhere in the volume. Since his many published texts hardly suggest that Yeats himself followed any rule consistently with respect to this minor concern, I have not listed the omissions.

A Full Moon in March:

P. 395: The first song should be printed in two four-line stanzas. (87E also in error here.)

The King of the Great Clock Tower:

P. 401, 11th line from bottom: A period should be placed after "out."

The Herne's Egg:

P. 407: Congal's last speech should end with a period.

P. 415: Second stage directions should read: ". . . Music, perhaps drum and concertina, to suggest breaking of wood. Enter, at the other side, the King. . . ."

P. 415, last line, and 416, 1st line: Should read: ". . . the table-leg . . . they fight, and the fight sways. . . ."

P. 417, 1. 2 of 1st stage directions: Should read ". . . near the throne and holds her egg towards it for a moment."

P. 423, next-to-last line: The comma after "cauldron" should be deleted.

Purgatory: The 7th line from the bottom of p. 433 should end with a period.

The Death of Cuchulain:

P. 439, l. 12: The comma should be replaced by a period.

P. 440, Cuchulain's 1st speech: Despite 87E, the semicolon should be replaced by the more logical colon of *Last Poems and Plays.*

P. 444: Again despite 87E, the Blind Man's 4th speech should end with a question mark, as in *Last Poems and Plays.*

Query: Should not "come," in l. 1 of the song on p. 229, be followed by a comma, as in some earlier editions?—And why any quotation marks at beginning and end if not also at beginning of second and third stanzas?